WALKS & TOURS

COPENHAGEN

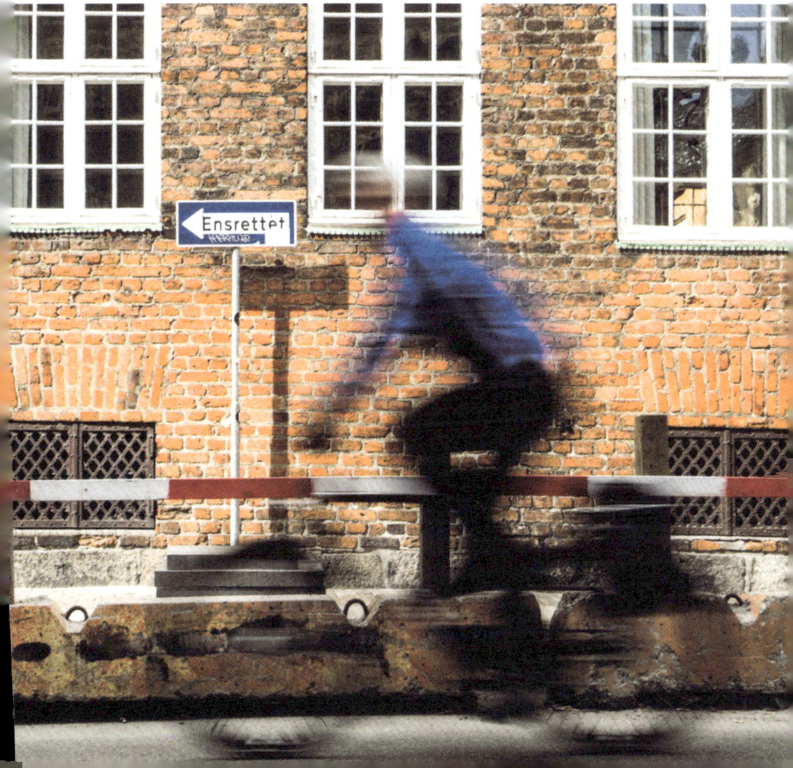

YOUR TAILOR-MADE TRIP STARTS HERE

Tailor-made trips and unique adventures crafted by local experts

Rough Guides has been inspiring travellers with lively and thought-provoking guidebooks for more than 35 years. Now we're linking you up with selected local experts to craft your dream trip. They will put together your perfect itinerary and book it at local rates.

Don't follow the crowd – find your own path.

HOW ROUGHGUIDES.COM/TRIPS WORKS

STEP 1

Pick your dream destination, tell us what you want and submit an enquiry.

STEP 2

Fill in a short form to tell your local expert about your dream trip and preferences.

STEP 3

Our local expert will craft your tailor-made itinerary. You'll be able to tweak and refine it until you're completely satisfied.

STEP 4

Book online with ease, pack your bags and enjoy the trip! Our local expert will be on hand 24/7 while you're on the road.

BENEFITS OF PLANNING AND BOOKING AT ROUGHGUIDES.COM/TRIPS

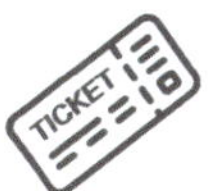

PLAN YOUR ADVENTURE WITH LOCAL EXPERTS

Rough Guides' English-speaking local experts are hand-picked, based on their experience in the travel industry and their impeccable standards of customer service.

SAVE TIME AND GET ACCESS TO LOCAL KNOWLEDGE

When a local expert plans your trip, you save time and money when you book, even during high season. You won't be charged for using a credit card either.

MAKE TRAVEL A BREEZE: BOOK WITH PEACE OF MIND

Enjoy stress-free travel when you use Rough Guides' secure online booking platform. All bookings come with a money-back guarantee.

WHAT DO OTHER TRAVELLERS THINK ABOUT ROUGH GUIDES TRIPS?

Trip to Spain

This Spain tour company did a fantastic job to make our dream trip perfect. We gave them our travel budget, told them where we would like to go, and they did all of the planning. Our drivers and tour guides were always on time and very knowledgable. The hotel accommodations were better than we would have found on our own. Only one time did we end up in a location that we had not intended to be in. We called the 24 hour phone number, and they immediately fixed the situation.

Don A, USA

Trip to Morocco

Our trip was fantastic! Transportation, accommodations, guides – all were well chosen! The hotels were well situated, well appointed and had helpful, friendly staff. All of the guides we had were very knowledgeable, patient, and flexible with our varied interests in the different sites. We particularly enjoyed the side trip to Tangier! Well done! The itinerary you arranged for us allowed maximum coverage of the country with time in each city for seeing the important places.

Sharon, USA

PLAN AND BOOK YOUR TRIP AT ROUGHGUIDES.COM/TRIPS

CONTENTS

Introduction

Trip plans

Directory

Art enthusiasts

Explore the National Gallery (walk 6), the Ny Carlsberg Glyptotek (walk 9), the Thorvaldsens Museum (walk 10) and Rosenborg (walk 5). Outside the city visit the Arken, Ørdrupgaard and Louisiana galleries (tour 14).

Best walks & tours for...

Children

Treat the kids to a trip to Tivoli (walk 9), day or night, and watch their fascination grow at the zoo (walk 8) or Experimentarium (walk 11). Be dazzled by the crown jewels at Rosenborg (walk 5).

Design Copenhagen

Lap up serious interiors inspiration at ahead-of-the-curve shop Illums Bolighus on Strøget (walk 2). The *Radisson Collection Royal* is a design icon (tour 1) and Designmuseum Danmark has thought-provoking displays (walk 4).

Food and wine

Copenhagen has fifteen Michelin-starred restaurants. Værnedamsvej (tour 1) is Copenhagen's gourmet food street, while Magasin du Nord (walk 3) offers an excellent food hall.

Hans Christian Andersen

Wander through the Danish author's stomping ground around Kongens Nytorv and Nyhavn (walk 3). Visit the Bakkehuset (tour 1), The Little Mermaid (tour 7) and the Church of Our Lady where his funeral was held (walk 2).

Renaissance architecture

Visit the Round Tower and Trinity Church (walk 2), Rosenborg Castle (walk 5), Kastellet and Nyboder (walk 4), the Stock Exchange (walk 10) and Christianshavn (walk 11).

Royalists

Follow in the footsteps of kings at Slotsholmen (walk 10), Rosenborg (walk 5), Church of Our Lady (walk 2), Amalienborg (walk 4) and Roskilde (tour 12). Don't miss the Royal Copenhagen store (walk 2).

Shoppers

Resist temptation in the department stores on Strøget (walk 2) and Kongens Nytorv (walk 3), the boutiques off Strøget, in Nørrebro (tour 7), and the independent shops in Vesterbro (tour 1).

INTRODUCTION

An introduction to Copenhagen and what makes it special, what not to miss and what to do when you're there.

Discover Copenhagen

Copenhagen is a pretty seaside city with a thriving nightlife, a sophisticated gastronomic and cultural scene, and a visible history going back nine hundred years.

Copenhagen (København), the capital of Denmark, is located on the eastern side of Sjælland (Zealand), the largest of Denmark's 407 (named) islands, with only the Øresund (Sound) separating it from Sweden. It was founded by Bishop Absalon in 1167, and these days, including its greater metropolitan area, is home to about 2.1 million of the country's estimated 5.7 million people. The smaller municipality of Copenhagen – made up of fifteen districts that extend beyond the geographical scope of this book – accounts for approximately 639,000 inhabitants.

Strategic link to Europe

Connected by the south of Jutland to Germany, Denmark is the only Scandinavian country physically joined to the European mainland and, as such, is the bridge between Scandinavia and the rest of the continent. It is also, quite literally, the bridge to Sweden, connected to the city of Malmö by the Øresund road and rail bridge.

Denmark shares many of the characteristics of its Nordic neighbours: liberal welfare benefits coupled with a high standard of living, and a style of government that aims at consensus and the avoidance of petty bureaucracy. Yet Denmark is also more accessible than the rest of Scandinavia, and its appeal is universal.

The city

With its strategic location at the mouth of the Baltic Sea, Copenhagen has always been an important hub and, as such, a tempting prize for pirates and traders. As a small fishing village in the twelfth century, it attracted the protection of Bishop Absalon and the dastardly attentions of Wendish pirates. One century later, German traders of the Hanseatic League were pounding on its doors. By the fifteenth century, the Sound was even more of a cash cow with its herring salted and exported all over Europe, and the king charging a toll on every ship that passed on its way to the Baltic.

Over the centuries, Copenhagen grew but always, even today, remained reasonably compact, its residents moving out gradually from the central core. In the twelfth century, Slotsholmen was the centre; by the Middle Ages, the town had expanded

Copenhagen has over 450km (280 miles) of cycle paths

across the water to the banks of what is now the Old Town.

The medieval citizens put up walls surrounded by a moat, which enclosed the city to the north, east and west. With the exception of Østerport (East Gate), which stood on Gothersgade until the seventeenth century, near to what is now Kongens Nytorv, the gates in the ramparts were on or near the sites still called Nørreport (North Gate) and Vesterport (West Gate). The fortress of Slotsholmen and the watery boundary of the Sound stood to the south. The five reservoirs to the north are all that remain of the medieval moat.

In the sixteenth century, under the aegis of Christian IV, the city's fortifications were extended east. The fortress Kastellet (see page 54) was built, and the East Gate and rampart were located next to it, thus bringing Rosenborg (1606–34) within the ramparts and practically doubling the amount of space within the city walls in what was known as 'New Copenhagen'. To the south, Christianshavn (see page 86) was built up, and a series of new islands created with naval yards and protective bastions. Nyboder, near Østerport, was constructed to house the naval workers. At the same time, Christian IV created some of the most lasting buildings of the entire city, including Rosenborg Castle, Kastellet, Børsen and the workers' district of Nyboder. Boasting an elegant Renaissance style, they are still standing today.

One century later, the city mushroomed again, as Frederiksstad (see page 49) was built in 'New Copenhagen' on the land acquired by Christian IV. It was (and is) the most aristocratic area in town, and was constructed on the site of a former royal country palace that had burnt down. On the banks of the Sound, Kongens Nytorv was developed and Nyhavn was excavated, and the merchants built their houses along its wharfs, to be close to the precious goods in their warehouses.

The Danes

Copenhagen's inhabitants are as appealing as their city; liberal, generally law-abiding, socially responsible (just look at their generous social security system, paid for with huge taxes that few complain about), gregarious, and – at the same time – charming and sarcastic. They are skilled at enjoying life, especially when it comes to *hygge*, a word that loosely translates as a combination of warmth, well-being and intimacy, usually involving the combination of family, friends and food. They are also informal in dealing with people and put a lot of focus on their personal freedom.

Copenhagen by night

Don't leave Copenhagen without...

Riding Tivoli's 100-year-old wooden rollercoaster. Tivoli pleasure gardens shelter one of the world's oldest rollercoasters. Even fuel rationing in World War II couldn't stop Rutschebanen from rolling along the tracks: all two tonnes of it were hauled to the top of the lift hill by hand. See page 79.

Sipping a cool beer on the 'sunny side' of Nyhavn. Colourful seventeenth-century houses and old wooden sailing ships provide the perfect backdrop for alfresco wining and dining. Nyhavn is an attractive street, often called Copenhagen's longest bar. See page 47.

Testing the next generation of city bikes. Found at docking stations around the city, Copenhagen's Bycyklen (https://bycyklen.dk) have built-in GPS and electric motors for when the pedalling gets tough. See page 134.

Winding your way to the top of the Rundetårn. This seventeenth-century astronomical observatory is a one-of-a-kind structure, set among the cobbled maze of Copenhagen's beautiful old Latin Quarter. See page 41.

Exploring the Louisiana Museum of Modern Art. Denmark's most-visited museum is a work of art in itself, its beautifully designed buildings surrounded by a sculpture garden overlooking the sparkling sea. It has a fabulous international collection, including works by Picasso, Giacometti, Miró and Henry Moore, as well as homegrown favourites like Asger Jorn. See page 103.

Eating *smørrebrød*. The Danish open-faced rye-bread sandwich is a work of art, whether it's a modern miniaturised 'smushi' version or the country's favourite 'Stjerneskud' (Shooting Star). See page 17.

Seeing the filming locations of *Borgen* and *The Killing* on Slotsholmen. Christiansborg Slot, home of the Danish parliament as well as many museums, will seem very familiar to fans of DR's gripping television dramas. Nordic Noir Tours (www.nordicnoirtours.com) runs walking tours visiting locations of *The Killing*, *The Bridge* and *Borgen*. See page 80.

Climbing the tower of Vor Frelsers Kirke. A wooden staircase made up of four hundred steps twists its way around the outside of the church's Baroque spire, becoming narrower and narrower as it does so. Not for anyone with vertigo, but the surefooted and clearheaded will be rewarded with spectacular city views. See page 88.

Taking a dip in the harbour. If you were hypnotised by the glittering water after taking a boat tour of Copenhagen's waterways (see page 48), grab your swimsuit and head for the open-air Islands Brygge harbour baths. See page 24.

Looking down on pedestrianized Strøget

Fire was always a threat in a town made of wood, and the eighteenth century saw two shocking blazes that destroyed almost the entire medieval centre. With the odd exception (including, fortunately, most of Christian IV's marvellous buildings), what the visitor sees today is eighteenth-century Neoclassical architecture.

By the nineteenth century, Copenhagen was too compact: it was packed with people and had no sanitation to speak of; certainly not enough to deal with the effluence that the heaving city spat out daily. In 1853, cholera broke out, killing several thousand people, including the well-known Golden-Age artist, Christoffer Eckersberg.

In 1856, the old ramparts were pulled down to improve conditions, and the populace spread into the countryside, which soon became the districts of Nørrebro, Vesterbro, Østerbro and Frederiksberg (although this is still technically a separate municipality from Copenhagen).

Thanks to the architect and town planner Ferdinand Meldahl (1827–1908), these districts were conserved as the parks that ring the inner city today, stretching from Kastellet, via Østre Anlæg behind the National Gallery of Art, the Botanical Gardens and Ørsteds Parken. Tivoli, also once part of the ramparts, was the work of entrepreneur George Carsten in 1843 (see page 79).

Modern Copenhagen

The twentieth and twenty-first centuries have seen a flurry of further changes to the city. The old quarter was pedestrianised from the 1960s; the docks are being rejuvenated; and the authorities have taken a particular interest in updating the city's landscape with startling modern structures such as the Black Diamond library extension (1999), the Harbour Baths (2003–11), the Opera House (2005), the Royal Danish Playhouse (2008), the DR Koncerthuset (2009), the Blue Planet aquarium (2013) and the Cirkelbroen (circle) bridge (2015). A whole new 'downtown' area, Ørestad, has been created from scratch on Amager island, and other areas of the suburbs are undergoing huge regeneration. Another ambitious project is the expansion of the Metro. The circular Cityringen line, made up of 15.5km (9.6 miles) of track with seventeen new stations, opened in 2019. Many of the city's most weird and wonderful designs were dreamed up by innovative architecture firm BIG Copenhagen (www.big.dk) – see its website for future plans.

Copenhagen districts

Indre By, the inner city covering an area of nine square kilometres (2200 acres), has a population of *c.*56,000. The quietest part of the Old Town is the financial district behind Kongens Nytorv and Holmens Kanal, where

Café culture

The Botanical Gardens

fewer than five hundred people live – there are generally more visitors gently snoring away every night than there are locals. More than half the apartments in this area are occupied by affluent young singles. They're also popular with those in the fifty-plus age bracket, who want to be close to the city centre's cultural opportunities.

Students and young families tend to live in Nørrebro or Vesterbro, which are also Copenhagen's most multicultural areas. Nørrebro has a population of almost 80,000 and is the most densely populated district. In recent years, it has seen more social problems than other parts of the city; nonetheless, it has the reputation for being a cool hangout. Once-seedy Vesterbro is now respectably edgy: over the past few years, a young creative crowd has moved in and transformed the old meatpacking district, Kødbyen, into a hub of stylish new bars, clubs, restaurants and galleries.

Christianshavn is Copenhagen's little Amsterdam, surrounded by water. The arrival of affluent newcomers attracted by a wave of recent regeneration has caused some resentment among the locals.

Østerbro and Frederiksberg are more upmarket; there are several embassies in Østerbro, including those of the US, Canada, Great Britain and Russia.

An eco-friendly city

These days, Copenhagen is still a compact city and, for the visitor, navigable on foot or by bike. The Danes cycle in their thousands: it makes for a city with clear air, fewer traffic jams, healthier people and the satisfaction of doing something good for the planet.

Copenhagen has a deserved reputation as the most bicycle-friendly city in the world. Forty-one percent of all journeys are made by bike, and there are over 450km (280 miles) of cycle paths, with even more planned. Special carriages for bikes on trains enable cyclists to combine biking with travelling on public transport more easily.

The emphasis on being eco-friendly becomes clear before you even set foot in Copenhagen. Look out of the plane as you approach the airport, and you can't fail to notice the massive Middelgrunden wind farm – the world's biggest when it opened in 2000 – in the Sound. Wind turbines such as these supply around 41 percent of all Denmark's electricity. The Sound itself is clean enough to swim in, and many of its beaches have been awarded Blue Flag status. The city authorities are very active: they have decreed that ninety percent of all food served in Copenhagen's public institutions should be organic – by 2024 the ninety percent mark had been reached – and that all citizens should be able to walk to a park in under fifteen minutes. Copenhagen also has a very ambitious programme of recycling, with plans to limit non-recyclable materials to two percent of household waste.

The Black Diamond, Slotsholmen

Top tips for exploring Copenhagen

Current events. For up-to-date Copenhagen listings, check out the Visit Copenhagen tourist office website (www.visitcopenhagen.com), or pick up a copy of the free weekly English-language newspaper, *The Copenhagen Post* (www.cphpost.dk), available from tourist offices and some hostels.

Free attractions. Entry is free for the under-18s to some museums, including the National Museum and the Hirschsprung Collection. There is free admission on Wednesdays to the Thorvaldsens Museum, and on Tuesdays to the Ny Carlsberg Glyptotek. It costs nothing to look at the statue of the Little Mermaid, people-watch in Christiania, or swim and sunbathe at Amager Beach. Copenhagen has some lovely parks and gardens where you can wander at will, including those around Rosenborg Castle, the nearby Botanical Gardens and romantic Frederiksberg Gardens.

Copenhagen Card. If you have kids in tow and plan to see a lot of sights, the Copenhagen Card (www.copenhagen card.com) is very good value; it allows free transport and entry to sights for up to two children under the age of ten for every adult card. There are also children's cards available for 10- to 15-year-olds.

Changing of the Guard. Amalienborg Palace is guarded by the Royal Life Guards *(Den Kongelige Livgarde)*. At around 11.30am each day, the guards march from their barracks at Gothersgade 100 (by Rosenborg Castle) to Amalienborg, where the Changing of the Guard ceremony takes place at noon.

Plan ahead for Roskilde Festival. Tickets to Northern Europe's biggest music festival, held in late June/early July, go on sale from 1 December.

Bring comfy shoes. The best way to see Copenhagen is by walking, but all those cobbles can be hard on the feet – make sure you bring suitable footwear for a blister-free visit.

Look out for bicycles. It might sound obvious, but pedestrians should take care when crossing cycle lanes. Copenhageners peddle fast, and if you aren't paying attention, you could easily cause an accident.

Tipping. While tipping is not the norm, no-one will complain if you reward excellent service.

Free wi-fi. Most cafés, bars and hotels across the city have free wi-fi, as does the Copenhagen Visitor Centre at Vesterbrogade 4A, across from Tivoli Gardens.

Go green. Copenhagen aims to become the world's first carbon-neutral city by 2025. The Discover Green Copenhagen map, available at tourist offices (www.visitcopenhagen.com), shows you where to find eco-friendly restaurants, cafés, hotels and shops.

Food and drink

Denmark is a gastronome's delight. Try beautifully prepared *smørrebrød*, or treat yourself to a New Nordic tasting menu – Copenhagen now has more Michelin-starred restaurants than any other city in Scandinavia.

Traditional Danish food, as you would expect from a seafaring nation in a cold, murky climate, was based around sturdy, filling dishes of carbohydrates, meat and fish. In this generally agricultural and maritime nation, people produced food from what they grew themselves or was available locally, using ingredients such as apples, beer, bread, cereals, carrots, dairy products, pork, onions, plums, potatoes and seafood. Dishes were seasonal in spring and summer but in the long, cold, dark winters, they depended on ingredients that had been preserved from the harvest seasons, using techniques such as pickling and salting. In the days of no refrigeration, it was these foods – ones that could be stored almost indefinitely – that came to dominate the country's traditional dishes.

These days, Danish food, especially in restaurants, has lightened up. Leading the charge is a generation of young chefs who are proponents of the New Nordic Cuisine manifesto, with its emphasis on showcasing the bounty of northern Europe by using local, organic, seasonal produce. Armed with these fresh ingredients, some have reinvented traditional Danish dishes for a modern palate, while others have combined them with flavours and culinary influences from abroad to create a new fusion cuisine (especially French, Italian and Thai).

Daily meals

A traditional Danish breakfast, or *morgenmad*, involves bread and butter, cheese, possibly cold meats and coffee. Porridge and beer-and-bread porridge *(øllebrød)* are very occasionally eaten. Of course, many people also eat cereal. Coffee is generally drunk rather than tea. In a hotel, the sheer scope of choice can be overwhelming, especially if faced with plates and plates of small Danish pastries *(wienerbrød)*.

Lunch, or *frokost*, can vary, but most people have an open sandwich or *smørrebrød*. This is traditionally a piece of dark rye bread with a topping. These can be quite complicated: *dyrlægens natmad* ('veterinarian's midnight snack'), for example, consists of liver paté *(leverpostej)*, topped with corned beef *(salt kød)* and a slice of meat aspic *(sky)*, and scattered with raw onion rings and cress.

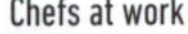

Chefs at work

Other popular sandwich toppings include smoked eel, scrambled egg and radishes; chopped liver paté with bacon and sautéed mushrooms; thin slices of roast pork *(ribbensteg)* with red sweet-and-sour cabbage; *gravadlax*, slices of smoked or cured salmon on white bread with shrimp, lemon and fresh dill; and, perhaps most complex of all, *stjerneskud* ('shooting star'), which consists of two pieces of fish (one steamed, one fried and battered) on a slab of buttered white bread, piled high with shrimp, mayonnaise, red caviar and a slice of lemon.

A classic alternative to *smørrebrød* is to eat from a *Dansk kold bord*, or Danish cold table. Some restaurants offer these, though it is very typical at home on festive occasions. The cold table is like a buffet, with a cold first course, usually some sort of marinated herring *(marinerede sild)*, which might be pickled or served in a red or white vinegar dressing. Sour cream sauces are also popular. On festive occasions, the herring might be prepared with other ingredients, such as potato, onions and capers topped with a dill sour cream/mayonnaise sauce. Herring is usually served with ice-cold snaps, which, according to the Danes, helps it to swim down to the stomach. Danish snaps *(akvavit)* is usually flavoured with caraway seed, at least 75 percent proof, and tends to be cheaper than imported spirits.

The second course will be cold meats and salads, followed by a warm dish, usually on a piece of rye bread, followed by cheese and biscuits.

Supper is called *middag* because it used to be eaten in the middle of the day. It is eaten at home and most Danes make an effort to gather the family around a hot meal every evening. Meat is usually served, often with traditional gravy and potato dishes, although international foods, such as pasta, pizza and American-influenced foods are also popular.

Culinary traditions

Food plays an important part both in Danish culture, as it brings people together, and in the concept of *hygge*, a term hard to translate but meaning something along the lines of 'cosiness, warmth and comfort with good food, drink and company', although it can mean different things to different people. Eating together is an important social event, whether it is a daily family affair or a dinner with non-family guests.

As in most places, there are times of year that the family comes together if it can. In Denmark, a Christmas lunch *(Julefrokost)* and an Easter lunch *(Påskefrokost)* are traditional. The Christmas table or *Julebordet* is organised like a *Kold Bord*, and, in addition to everyday *smørrebrød* toppings, there will be special dishes such as *æbleflæsk* (pork slices served with an apple, onion

Traditional smørrebrød

A delicate starter at Studio

and bacon compote), *flæskesteg* (roast pork with crackling) and *Julesylte*, a pork paté accompanied by pickled beetroot and mustard.

Other festive foods include goose (though many people now prefer duck), eaten on 24 December with boiled potatoes, pickled red cabbage, tiny caramelised potatoes and gravy and, for pudding, *Ris à l'amande*, a rice pudding served with whipped cream, chopped almonds and cherry sauce. Traditionally, everyone eats until someone finds the whole almond hidden in the pudding. This dish was served first as, in the past, it was used to fill everyone up, so that a small amount of meat would go around. The meal is usually washed down with beer or *snaps*.

Restaurant scene

In Copenhagen, there are over two thousand restaurants and cafés, which will usually provide a good meal. There are also those that will provide something extraordinary: fifteen restaurants were awarded 26 Michelin stars in 2024. With three Michelin stars under his belt, *Geranium*'s chef Rasmus Kofoed is currently the city's brightest culinary star while René Redzepi's *Noma* topped the revered World's 50 Best Restaurants list for the third time in 2021.

Copenhagen's cafés are usually open from the morning until late at night, and make especially cosy corners for curling up with coffee and cake. Most serve alcohol and will provide food throughout the day and into the evening, and some turn into clubs with music and dancing at night. If you prefer bartenders to baristas, cocktail joints have become very popular in recent years – plump for a 1920s classic or experiment with contemporary creations such as the Spotted Pig (at *Salon 39*; Vodroffsvej 39) or the rum-based Ruby Daiquiri (at *Ruby*; Nybrogade 10).

Restaurants are usually more formal, and the kitchen will close a couple of hours before the last people are expected to leave. If you want to eat late, always ring to find out when the kitchen closes. Places that dish up both lunch and supper often stop serving in the late afternoon, so don't be surprised if lunch is not available after 2pm. For smart restaurants, it is always advisable to book ahead.

Foodie shops

Copenhagen has some excellent food stores. Dubbed a 'gourmet street', Vesterbro's **Værnedamsvej** is a wonderful place to find delicatessens, a high-quality butcher, greengrocer, and wine, cheese and chocolate shops. If you don't venture that far, all the department stores shelter an upmarket grocery.

For organic bread, pâtisseries, wine, chocolate and oil, check out one of the many **Emmerys** stores (central outlets

A feast for the eyes and the tastebuds

include Ved Vesterport 3; Vestergade 13; Store Strandstraede 21; www.emmerys.dk). A new wave of organic delicatessens includes the renowned **Meyers Deli** (Kattegatvej 53; www.meyersmad.dk). Those with a sweet tooth should head for one of the **Lagkagehuset** pâtisseries (http://lagkagehuset.dk) to sample Danish cakes and pastries. A growing crop of microbreweries offers thirsty travellers pilsner-type beers, from Tivoli's own **Færgekroen Bryghus** (Vesterbrogade 3; http://faergekroen.mikkeller.com) to the prize-winning **Nørrebro Bryghus** (Ryesgade 3; www.noerrebrobryghus.dk).

The city's biggest indoor market, Torvehallerne, near Nørreport metro station, has over sixty stalls selling fresh produce, as well as sushi, tapas and porridge stands.

The *pølsevogn* (sausage wagon) is a fast-food institution in Copenhagen. Hotdogs, including the infamous long red *røde pølser* sausages are slathered in mustard, ketchup and remoulade, and washed down with chocolate milk.

Traditional dishes

Æbleflæsk Pork slices with an apple, onion and bacon compote.
Æggekage 'egg cake', a substantial omelette-like dish, sometimes made with flour so it rises slightly.
Biksemad Beef hash topped with a fried egg and a dollop of ketchup.
Blodpølse Black pudding, made from pig's blood.
Brændende kærlighed 'burning love', mashed potato with fried onion and pieces of bacon.
Finker Sweetmeat similar to haggis.
Flæskesteg Roast pork with crackling *(svær)*.
Frikadeller Meatballs, Denmark's 'national' dish.
Millionbøf Tiny pieces of beef in gravy, poured over mashed potato. The name means 'million steak'.
Øllebrød Porridge made with rye bread, sugar and beer.
Stegte sild i eddike Fried herring in vinegar.

Eco-labelling

The Danish mark of inspection for organic products is a red 'Ø' symbol. This indicates that the product has been inspected by the Danish authorities and must meet stringent quality and production regulations. A product can only be marketed as organic if 95 percent of its ingredients are certified by the 'Ø' symbol. The same criteria applies to foods bearing the 'Euro-leaf' logo, the EU's official organic label used throughout Europe.

The EU flower symbol and the Nordic Council of Ministers' stylised swan symbol are common eco-labels, used on non-food products that do not contain any toxic ingredients and that have been manufactured with the least possible impact to the environment.

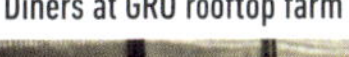

Diners at GRO rooftop farm

Shopping

Copenhagen is an appealing, if not especially cheap, place to shop, especially for Danish designer goods, particularly furniture, household items and clothing. Whether you buy or not, it's a great place for window-shopping.

The shopping map

With plenty of cafés and street entertainment, and over a kilometre of pedestrianised streets, Strøget makes for a fun shopping experience. The quality of the goods in its mainstream shops improves as you head up the street from Rådhuspladsen, reaching a smart conclusion up by Kongens Nytorv, with designer boutiques and furriers such as Prada, Gucci and Louis Vuitton, and Danish designers SAND and Birger Christensen.

Vimmelskaftet, Amagertorv and Østergade are home to some of Denmark's most famous names. Here you'll find Lego's flagship emporium; the 120-year-old department store Illums; its sister store, Illums Bolighus, which will fulfil all your designer desires for household gadgets and Danish furniture and lighting; Royal Copenhagen, with its world-famous china (and the opportunity to paint your own plate or cup, see page 39); Georg Jensen, the father of simply designed silver jewellery (at a price); and Hay House, an important stop for minimalist furniture and colourful rugs.

Magasin du Nord, an elegant department store located on Kongens Nytorv, will take care of your sartorial needs. Up the road, Danish audio wizards Bang & Olufsen has its main store.

Do not be afraid to wander off Strøget into the streets adjoining it, as it is here that you'll stumble across independently owned, quirky little shops. Tucked off the main thoroughfare are gems such as Stilleben at Niels Hemmingsensgade 3, which sells unusual homeware and handmade ceramics; or Norse Store at Pilestræde 41, a must for fashion-conscious chaps.

Farvergade, Kompagnistræde and Laederstræde run parallel to Strøget in one uninterrupted pedestrian street, lined with shops dealing in Persian rugs, antique furniture, silverware, china and curios. The prices aren't exactly low, but on a good day it's possible to find a fair deal. These streets are more popular than Strøget among Copenhageners and the cafés are always full of people. Hidden away in a basement at No. 5 Læderstræde is Wettergren & Wettergren, whose owners update vintage clothing and

The world-famous Egg chair designed by Arne Jacobsen

accessories. For presents, such as pastel porcelain and flowery cushions, try Liebe at No. 23 Kompagnistræde.

The Latin Quarter, close to the university, is littered with bookshops *(boghandel)* and second-hand clothing and record shops. There are flower stalls round the back of Magasin du Nord; for a more exotic floral experience, peek in the window of designer florist Tage Andersen at Ny Adelgade 12.

Kronprinsensgade, north of Strøget, shelters many of Denmark's designer clothes shops, like the exclusive Stig P at No. 14.

Away from the centre

Elsewhere, there are plenty of opportunities to seek out independent little shops. Out in Nørrebro, for example, around Sankt Hans Torv, you will find antique and bric-a-brac shops on Ravensborggade; vintage clothing on Blågardsgade; and young, eclectic clothes shops run by aspiring designers in streets such as Elmegade – try design collective Fünf at No. 2, Stokkel at No. 3 for shoes and accessories, or Radical Zoo at No. 19 for edgier Danish fashion.

Nansensgade near the reservoirs is an up-and-coming area, with a smattering of interesting shops and cafés.

Better still is trendy Vesterbro: Istedgade boasts a cluster of boutiques run by emerging artists and designers, some still experimenting with their styles. Longstanding favourites include Donn Ya Doll at No. 55, with a mouthwatering choice of thirty clothes designers; and Kyoto at No. 95, with a cool selection of understated Scandinavian fashion. In the same district, Designer Zoo (Vesterbrogade 137) showcases the creations of seven Danish designers, who work on the premises in glass, ceramics, wool and gold, plus changing works from twenty to forty invited artists.

If you are after authentic antiques, Bredgade near the Amalienborg is full of shops and auction houses. However, the largest destination for antiques is Green Square in Amager (Strandlodsvej 11B).

Danish interior design

Danish furniture ranks among the world's best and has become increasingly popular. Here you'll see items credited to the designer rather than to the factory. Furniture is a national pride, and most good pieces will have a black circular 'Danish furniture-makers' sticker attached. Lamps are also lovingly designed, as are household textiles and handwoven rugs.

If you want your shops under one roof, the best places are Illums Bolighus (Amagertorv 10; www.illumsbolighus.com), Casa (Store Regnegade 2; www.casashop.dk) or, north of Osterbrø, designer furniture store Paustian (Kalkbrænderiløbskaj 2; www.paustian.com).

Inside the Copenhagen-based Munthe plus Simonsen store

Culture and nightlife

There is lots to do in the evenings in Copenhagen, above and beyond eating out. This section features general information about the main concert venues and nightlife hotspots; for individual bar and club listings, see page 122.

Tivoli

An evening visit to **Tivoli** (see page 79) is a must, even if it is just for a wander to take in the lights, fireworks and atmosphere. If you wish to be a little more focussed, the open-air stage hosts free evening concerts on Fridays. There is also an impressive concert hall, with an aquarium in the foyer.

Concert halls

The **Tivoli Concert Hall** (www.tivoli.dk) is one of the largest venues for ballet, opera and classical music in Copenhagen; it also stages rock concerts and is a major venue during the jazz festival in July. You will need to book in advance.

The Danish Symphony Orchestra were treated to a fabulous new home in 2009: the **DR Koncerthuset** (Emil Holms Kanal 20; https://drkoncerthuset.dk) on Amager, designed by Frenchman Jean Nouvel, is a jaw-dropping piece of architecture and the most expensive concert hall ever built. Its spaces are used for pop, rock and jazz as well as classical concerts.

Theatre, opera and dance

There are several venues for theatre, opera and dance in Copenhagen – some more dependent on an understanding of Danish than others. **The Opera House** (Operaen; Ekvipagemestervej 10, Holmen; https://kglteater.dk; see page 90) offers both traditional and modern opera and ballet in a startling building. The auditorium is very comfortable with excellent visibility and acoustics. Ticket prices vary from 150dkk in the gods to 1000dkk in the stalls.

Its sister venue, the **Royal Theatre** (Det Kongelige Teater; https://kglteater.dk) puts on some concerts and ballets, but its functions have mostly been superseded by the Opera House and the more modern **Royal Danish Playhouse** (Skuespilhuset; Kvæsthusbroen; www.kglteater.dk), on the waterfront near Nyhavn. It has two big stages – the main stage with 650 seats and Portscenen with two hundred seats – as well as the smaller Store Scene, together with a studio stage, restaurant, café and a large public square in front of the building with harbour views. For some performances

The Royal Theatre stalls

the north wall can be opened up on to the quayside. Almost half the building is constructed in the water, partly on new fill and partly on detached piles.

The **New Theatre** (Det Ny Teater; Gammel Kongevej 29; www.detnyteater.dk), just off Vesterbrogade, does a roaring trade in big-name musicals such as *West Side Story*, *My Fair Lady*, *Phantom of the Opera* and *Beauty and the Beast*.

Jazz clubs and dinner dances

Copenhagen has a bit of a reputation for jazz, with a renowned ten-day international festival held from the first Friday of July onwards. The **Copenhagen Jazz House** (http://jazzhouse.dk), the city's premier jazz spot; Jazz House Montmartre (www.jazzhusmontmartre.dk); and the smaller, more intimate **Mojo's** (https://mojo.dk) should tide you over until festival time.

If you fancy an all-in-one bit of entertainment, try out **Wallmans Saloner** (Cirkusbygningen, Jernbanegade 8; www.wallmans.dk; prices from 500dkk), where your evening takes in a four-course meal and stage entertainment (dancers, singers and acrobats), followed by a night of dancing.

Bars and clubs

Copenhagen has plenty of cool drinking places, from rustic bistros to chic modern bars to cosy cellar pubs. Danes take pride in their lager-style beers, and there are several excellent brewpubs, such as **Nørrebro Bryghus**, where you can sample beer made on the premises. Copenhageners love a cocktail – you'll find plenty of shaking and stirring going on around town.

There is no shortage of places to dance the night away, including many late-opening cafés and bars. **Vega**, in Vesterbro, is one of the oldest and biggest nightclubs. Vesterbro is also where you'll find the former butchers' district Kødbyen, which has seen an incredible reinvention over the past few years and is now one of the city's hottest areas for wining, dining and partying. New places are still opening there, such as the massive KBIII nightclub. The city's edgier neighbourhoods, such as Nørrebro, have a large share of up-and-coming bars, and grungier clubs such as **Rust**, which hosts live bands and international DJs.

Of course, the best parties are the ones that you stumble upon accidentally – ask the locals.

Listings

For listings of what's going on in Copenhagen, including cinema listings (most films are shown in their original version with subtitles), check out The Copenhagen Post (www.cphpost.dk), the English-language weekly newspaper. Visit Copenhagen (www.visitcopenhagen.com) also has a diary of events.

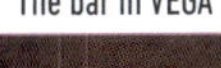

The bar in VEGA

Sports and outdoor activities

Copenhagen has activities to suit every taste, from open-air swimming in the summer to ice-skating in the winter. The top spectator sport is football, while popular participation sports often involve water.

Swimming

There are about a dozen indoor swimming pools in Copenhagen, some with sauna, massage and gym facilities, and several open-air pools which are usually open from June to August. So successful has the clean-up of the Inner Harbour been that there is now a fantastically popular outdoor bathing area at Islands Brygge (open June to August), with five pools (two just for kids), three diving towers and a green lawn packed full of picnickers in front. In Sluseholmen you can swim at Fisketorvet and Havnebadet (both open June to August; http://svoemkbh.kk.dk).

Five kilometres (three miles) south of the city centre, Amager Strandpark (http://international.kk.dk) is a vast artificial beach and lagoon, where Copenhageners flock to swim, run, row, skate, and play beach volleyball. There are Metro stations at three places along the beach: Øresund, Amager Strand and Femøren.

Last but not least, the sandy Svanemølle Beach and its 130-metre (423ft) -long pier in Østerbro. The beach has lifeguards during July and August.

Watersports

Kayaking and boat hire

You can hire kayaks from Kayak Republic (http://kayakrepublic.dk), based near Holmens Kirke, to explore the city's canals (guided tours are also available). Groups of six or more can try their hand at kayak polo – contact Kayakklub (http://amagerroog kajakklub.dk) at Amager Strandpark. Also at Amager Strandpark, you can rent kayaks and canoes from Kajakhotellet (https://kajakhotellet.dk).

Another eco-friendly option is to hire one of the solar-powered picnic boats from GoBoat (www.goboat.dk), situated next to the Islands Brygge swimming pools. These cute little crafts chug along the city's canals at a leisurely three knots.

Wakeboarding and kitesurfing

You can learn to wakeboard in a safe environment at Kabelparken (http://copenhagencablepark.dk; open June to August); or if you already have the skills, you can take to the water for 350dkk per hour (including gear). You can also hire equipment and take kite-surfing lessons with KiteCPH (http://kitecph.dk), based at Amager Strandpark.

A solar-powered GoBoat

Ice-skating

Numerous stretches of water within the capital's boundaries freeze over in winter and outdoor rinks *(skøjtebaner)* are set up at Frederiksberg Runddel and Kongens Nytorv. The biggest outdoor ice-skating rink in Northern Europe can be found in Genforeningspladsen, 4km (2.5 miles) northwest of the city centre – skate rental is available daily in winter until 8pm.

Activity tours

If trudging round after an umbrella-waving guide feels too slow, pick up the pace with an activity tour. Running Copenhagen (https://running copenhagen.com) has various themed tours, including an interesting route focusing on the city's architecture – you'll need an average running speed of six minutes per kilometre if you want to keep up. Running Tours Copenhagen (www.runningtours.dk) visits similar places and can tailor tours to individuals for a slightly higher price.

In Copenhagen, cycling is a way of life. You can easily hire a bike (see page 134) and set out on your own, but many companies offer guided explorations of the city – try Cycling Copenhagen (www.cycling-copenhagen.dk) or Bike Copenhagen with Mike (http://bikecopenhagenwithmike.dk). Mountain bikers can head for the purpose-built 26km (16-mile) trail network in Hareskoven woods, 14km (9 miles) northwest of the city, either under their own pedal-power or with a guide from MTB Tours (http://mtb-tours.dk).

Mountain of rubbish

Denmark is hardly the hilliest of countries; but if you can't go to the mountain, you must bring the mountain to you. Amager Bakke/ Copenhill is (www.a-r-c.dk) an innovative year-round ski and hiking slope plus climbing wall all on the roof of a waste incinerator – a perfect example of when sustainability is fun.

Spectator sports

Football

The Danish football team competes at the highest level, and the sport has an enthusiastic following. The main Copenhagen stadium is at Parken (www.teliaparken.dk), and is often used for major international matches. It is also the home ground of F.C. Copenhagen, the most successful club in Danish league football.

Handball

In winter, handball is the country's official game. The successful KIF Kolding København team play at Sydbank Arena Kolding sports arena (www.koldinghallerne.dk) or EWII Arena Brøndby (http://brondbyhallen.dk), depending on fixtures. Tickets can be purchased from www.billetlugen.dk.

Exploring the harbour by kayak

Chronology

An expanding and contracting economic and political power, Denmark has, in its time, ruled over much of Europe and Scandinavia. It is now an independent-minded member of the EU.

Viking period

***c.*AD 700–1000** The Vikings colonise Britain, Normandy and much of southern Sweden, and also reach Greenland, Canada, North Africa, Russia and Constantinople.
960 Harald Bluetooth converts to Christianity.

Middle Ages

1157 Valdemar I accedes to the throne and unifies Denmark after a century of unrest.
***c.*1160** Bishop Absalon builds the first castle on Slotsholmen.
1254 Købmandshavn (Copenhagen) receives a charter.
1282 Danish nobles force the unpopular king Erik V to sign the Great Charter at Nyborg, limiting his authority.
1397 Margrethe I (1375–1412) sets up the Kalmar Union, an alliance with Norway and Sweden, in which Denmark rules all three.
1417 Margrethe's grandnephew, Erik VII, builds Kronborg Castle at Helsingør, a fortress and 'toll booth' to collect money from ships.
1425–79 Copenhagen flourishes and grows. In 1443, it becomes Denmark's capital and in 1479, Copenhagen University is founded.

Renaissance

1523 The Kalmar Union ends with Gustav Vasa's coronation as King of Sweden. Norway remains part of Denmark until 1814.
1536 The Reformation: Denmark becomes a Protestant country.
1588–1648 Copenhagen booms and the city expands in the sixty-year reign of Christian IV but Denmark's entry (1625–29) into the Thirty Years' War (1618–48) against the Holy Roman Empire is a costly disaster.
1658–59 Denmark loses another war with Sweden, ceding a third of its territories, including control over the profitable Sound.

Eighteenth and nineteenth centuries

1711–12 Plague claims a third of Copenhagen's population.
1728 Major fires gut much of the city leading to reconstruction.
1754 The Royal Danish Academy of Art is founded, inspiring a 'Golden Age' (1800–50) of the arts.

Sailing ships moored in Copenhagen in the late nineteenth century

1788 Serfdom is abolished.
1801–14 Neutral Copenhagen is bombarded by the English Navy to prevent her from doing business with France. Britain attacks again in 1807. Denmark sides with France and is bankrupt by 1813. Denmark loses Norway to Sweden in the Treaty of Kiel.
1848–9 Frederik VII abolishes absolute monarchy.
1864 After war with Prussia and Austria, Denmark cedes her territories of Schleswig and Holstein to Germany.

Twentieth and twenty-first centuries

1914–18 Denmark remains neutral during the World War I.
1929–40 Welfare state is set up under a left-wing coalition dominated by the Social Democrats. Economic depression in the 1930s.
1940–45 Neutral Denmark is invaded by Germany in 1940. It joins the Allies in 1943 and most of the Jewish population to safety in Sweden.
1968–71 Christiania is founded after student unrest.
1972 Margrethe II becomes queen.
1973 Denmark joins the EEC (EU).
1989 Denmark is the first country to recognise same-sex marriages.
2000 Denmark votes against the euro. The Øresund Bridge, a rail and road link with Sweden, opens.

Former prime minister Helle Thorning-Schmidt

2011 Helle Thorning-Schmidt, Denmark's first female prime minister, leads a centre-left coalition into power.
2015 Filmmaker Finn Noergaard and a security guard are killed in Copenhagen by an Islamist terrorist. Lars Lokke Rasmussen returns as PM at the helm of minority government led by his liberal Venstre party.
2016 Bikes outnumber cars in the centre of Copenhagen.
2020 Denmark wins praise for its response to the Covid-19 pandemic, with relatively low numbers of infection and deaths.
2024 Frederik X becomes king; the Danish Parliament agrees a major new green deal, limiting emissions and expanding the country's forests.

King Frederik X and Queen Mary of Denmark

RE CLAUS

TRIP PLANS

TOUR 1
Vesterbro

This route takes you from Central Station through Vesterbro, Copenhagen's former red-light district. Vesterbro retains its seamier edges, but is also one of the most vibrant parts of the city: Istedgade is packed with one-off boutiques, while the old butchers' quarter Kødbyen has a buzzing bar and restaurant scene.

DISTANCE: 5km (3 miles)
TIME: A half-/full day
START: Hovedbanegården
END: Bakkehuset
POINTS TO NOTE: This is quite a lengthy route. If you want to speed things up and possibly combine with all, or part of, the Frederiksberg Walk (see page 71), after Værnedamsvej, take the 6A bus down Vesterbrogade to Pile Allé (turn left for Carlsberg) or on to the zoo.

Until the mid-nineteenth century, Vesterbrogade, Vesterbro's main street, was the paved and busy road that led to Copenhagen's west gate, or 'Vesterport', through a rural area mainly put to pasture bar a few industrial buildings and timber yards. Until 1853, building outside the city walls was not allowed, except with express permission. However, with the rise of industrialisation, dreadful sanitation, increased pressure on living space within the city walls and a cholera outbreak in June 1853, which killed around 4500 people, this prohibition was lifted. In 1856, the city ramparts and gates were pulled down and construction began in earnest in all the 'bro' ('bridge') districts beyond the city.

Vesterbro was never an expensive area and when the red-light district in Pisserenden was cleared out in the early 1900s, many of its workers flocked here. Gentrification has well and truly taken root, with a wave of restoration projects and a growing crop of restaurants and bars springing up across the streets. Today, the neighbourhood is home to a creative community of young artists and designers and a thriving immigrant population. It has emerged as a cool district filled with quirky, unusual shops and buzzing cafés.

Outside the station

Start outside **Hovedbanegården** ❶, designed in 1911 by the prolific railway architect Heinrich Wenck, who drafted plans for 150 of Denmark's

Vesterbrogade

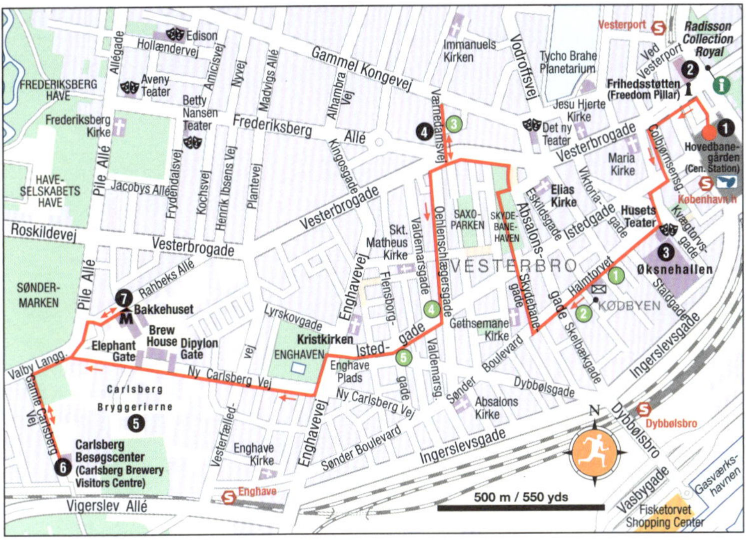

stations. The country's first railway line, built between 1847 and 1848, ran from here to Roskilde (see page 92).

The Freedom Pillar

Head towards the obelisk on Vesterbrogade. Unveiled in 1797, when it stood outside the city walls, the **Freedom Pillar** (Frihedstøtten) commemorates the end of adscription in 1788, which meant that peasants could leave the estate where they were born and choose to live and work elsewhere. Before this, they were legally tied to their feudal lord and could be hunted down, brought back and punished severely if they tried to leave. The four figures represent Loyalty, Civic Virtue, Cultivating the Soil and Valour.

Radisson Collection Royal

The tower block on the corner of Vesterbrogade and Hammerichsgade is the **Radisson Collection Royal** ❷, an iconic hotel in the history of architecture erected in 1960 by Arne Jacobsen (1902–71), the architect and designer credited with almost single-handedly creating the world's concept of practical but stylish Danish design. **Room 606** is the only one that retains Jacobsen's original interiors, but you can admire his famous 'Egg' and 'Swan' chairs in the lobby. The twentieth-

Hovedbanegården, Copenhagen's ornate central railway station

Carlsberg beer

The Carlsberg brewery was set up by ale-brewer Jacob Christian Jacobsen (1811–87) in 1847, the year that he produced his first commercial beer using the new German lagering process. He named the brewery after his five-year-old son Carl; 'berg' refers to the hill on which it was built. Carl built a second brewery close by in 1882 and took the ancient swastika symbol as the new Carlsberg trademark. Both father and son espoused perfection, Jacobsen *père* even citing it in his will, 'In working the brewery it should be a constant purpose, regardless of immediate gain, to develop the art of making beer to the greatest possible degree of perfection'.

floor restaurant **Café Royal** provides wonderful meals and panoramic views.

Into Vesterbro

Turn left down Vesterbrogade, and left again onto Colbjørnsensgade. You are now in the former red-light area. After the brothels closed and sex workers moved out, an influx of young creatives, and hip bars and restaurants transformed the neighbourhood, though you'll still see a few strip clubs and sex shops. Turn right into Istedgade and left down Helgoslandgade into Halmtorvet, a former haymarket and now dotted with cafés. Opposite, **Øksnehallen** ❸ (Halmtorvet 11; charge for exhibitions) is an old cattle market turned trade-fair and exhibition space.

Kødbyen

Stretching several blocks to the west, Kødbyen ('Meat Town') has reinvented itself as one of the city's most dynamic corners. The former cattle pens, slaughterhouses and market halls now shelter gallery spaces, creative companies, and the city's coolest bars, cafés and clubs. Stop here for lunch at one of the many excellent restaurants, such as the all-organic **Warpigs**, see ①, or pizzeria **Mother**, see ②; or bookmark the area and return after sundown to soak up the area's lively nightlife.

Continue down Halmtorvet and at Sønder Boulevard 73 take a look at the **Absalon community house**, set in a converted old church rebuilt by Lennart Lejboschitz, cofounder of the famous Tiger stores. Then retrace your steps and turn left six streets down into **Skydebanegade**. Walk past the yellow townhouses and cross the main road. Pass through the gate in the imposing brick wall opposite, which leads into **Skydebanehaven**. This park once belonged to the Royal Shooting Club, whose former mansion-like clubhouse, at the far end of the park, was one of the first buildings in Vesterbro. To reach the clubhouse, walk through the kids' play area and follow the path to the exit, turning left onto Absalonsgade, and left again onto Vesterbrogade.

Performance at Øsknehallen

Værnedamsvej

Continue along Vesterbrogade, to the junction with Frederiksberg Allé. Then, turn right up **Værnedamsvej** 4, famous for its gourmet shopping and a good place for lunch or early supper; try **Les Trois Cochons**, see 3. Once you've finished exploring the culinary riches of this tasty little street, return to Vesterbrogade and then cross the road into Oehlenschlægersgade where you will find, on the corner with Kaalundsgade, an extraordinary mosaic-covered building, reminiscent of Gaudí's work in Barcelona – all lovingly put together by the late Nigerian-born artist Manuel Tafat (1945–2006).

The Carlsberg Brewery

Continue to the end of the street and turn right along Istegade. If you fancy an afternoon coffee, there are several good cafés along here, notably **Bang and Jensen**, see 4, and **Riccos**, see 5. After passing four streets, turn left onto Enghavevej. Keep going and turn right at a large crossroads onto Ny Carlsberg Vej, where you are heading for the **Carlsberg Brewery** 5 (Carlsberg Bryggerierne). Note that the actual brewing of the lager takes place in an industrial estate in the suburbs.

Head for the archway in the distance. After crossing Væsterfælledvej, look to your left to see the tall **winding chimney** decorated with lotus flowers and gargoyles (copied from Notre-Dame in Paris). Carlsberg wanted to prove that an industrial chimney could be beautiful so commissioned one of Copenhagen's most celebrated architects, Vilhelm Dahlerup, to design this one in 1900.

The first archway, called the **Dipylon Gate**, was built in 1892 and originally housed two malting floors; malt was loaded in and out of carriages through tubes in the gate's ceiling. The figure group on the roof, by sculptor Stephen Sinding, is called *The Bell Strikers*. The mosaics on the other side of the gate show Carl Jacobsen, his wife Ottilia and son and heir Alf (who died in 1890); Vilhelm Dahlerup and master builder S.P. Beckmann; and four figures representing the brewery's employees.

Duck through the gate and you will see another archway held up by the four famous life-size **Carlsberg elephants**. They were partly inspired by the elephants holding up the organ in Our Saviour's Church (Vor Frelsers Kirke, see page 88) and partly by Bernini's obelisk-carrying elephant in Piazza Minerva in Rome. Note the copper busts of Carl and Ottilia Jacobsen peering down from a gallery at the top of the gate.

The Renaissance-style building on the right of the gate is the Brew House, with a balcony modelled on those in the Palazzo Bavilaque in Verona. On the roof is a large copper sculpture representing *Thor's Battle Against the Giants*. Walk under the 'Elephant Gate' to the end, passing, on your left, the Carlsberg Museum & Business Centre.

Inside the Carlsberg Brewery

Retro Carlsberg poster

Food and drink

1 Warpigs
Flæsketorvet 25–37;
http://warpigs.dk; €€
Part brewpub, part BBQ joint, this place serves great brisket and has a buzzing atmosphere, with a rock 'n' roll soundtrack.

2 Mother
Høkerboderne 9–15;
http://mother.dk; €
One of the city's favourite pizza places thanks to its cosy atmosphere and small, select menu of sourdough creations.

3 Les Trois Cochons
Værnedamsvej 10; www.cofoco.dk; €
This atmospheric, elegant old butcher's shop delivers both style and good food at an affordable price.

4 Bang and Jensen
Istedgade 130;
www.bangogjensen.dk/english; €
A former pharmacy reimagined as a cool, and very popular, café-bar. Particularly tasty brunches.

5 Riccos
Istedgade 119; www.riccos.dk; €
Café chain that churns out excellent coffee to weary passersby.

The Carlsberg Visitor Centre

Swerve left onto Valby Langgade and then take the first left into Gamle Carlsberg Vej, where about halfway down on the left you will find the **Carlsberg Visitor Centre** **6** (Carlsberg Besøgscenter; Gamle Carlsberg Vej 11; www.visitcarlsberg.dk; charge). These listed brewery buildings date from 1867, when they were rebuilt following a fire. The exhibition offers an interesting insight into brewing past and present and you can sample a pint in the airy bar.

Bakkehuset

Retrace your steps to the top of Ny Carlsberg Vej, continue down Pile Allé, then take the second right, Rahbeks Allé, to find the oldest building in the area. **Bakkehuset** **7** (Rahbeks Allé 23; http://frederiksbergmuseerne.dk/en/bakkehuset; charge) dates from the 1650s when it was an inn. From 1787, it was home to Kamma and Knud Lyne Rahbek, literary personalities of the nineteenth-century Golden Age (see page 60). It is now a cultural museum, furnished in a rather sparse romantic style. The poets Johannes Ewald (1743–81) and Adam Oehlenschläger (1779–1850), are featured and there is also memorabilia relating to Hans Christian Andersen (1805–75; see page 58).

Continue down Rahbeks Allé to Vesterbrogade, where you can pick up the 6A bus back into town or a train from Carlsberg station.

An old cart used to transport beer out of the brewery

WALK 2
The old inner city

This circular walk takes you through the oldest part of Copenhagen and encompasses Strøget, the world's longest pedestrianised street, Gammel Strand (Old Beach) and the University or Latin Quarter. It is now a lively district brimming with shops, bars and restaurants.

DISTANCE: 3.5km (2 miles)
TIME: A half-/full day
START/END: Rådhuspladsen
POINTS TO NOTE: This walk takes quite a while if you visit everything. However, if you want to combine part of it with other walks, from Højbro Plads you can visit Slotsholmen (see page 80) or continue down Strøget to Kongens Nytorv and Nyhavn (see pages 45 and 47).

With the exception of Slotsholmen (see page 80), this is the oldest part of Copenhagen. Predominantly built in wood, the old city was a martyr to fire and almost completely demolished in 1728 and 1795. The first fire razed nearly fifty percent of the medieval city and destroyed the homes of around twenty percent of the population; the second pretty much finished off the job. So, although the area has been inhabited for over seven hundred years, there are very few buildings that remain from before the eighteenth century.

Start at Rådhuspladsen (see page 78), which was built in the nineteenth century just inside the old city walls (now demolished), and walk down Frederiksberggade, one of the five streets that make up **Strøget** (literally 'stripe' and pronounced 'stroll'), the world's longest pedestrianised street, which reaches all the way to royal Kongens Nytorv (see page 45) by the harbour.

This western end of Strøget is the least sophisticated part, characterised by fast-food joints and fast-fashion stores, in contrast with the middle and final stretches, where you will find Danish design and top fashion brands.

Gammeltorv

Follow the cobbles to the first large open area that you come to. This is the site of Havn, Copenhagen's oldest village. **Gammeltorv** ❶ (Old Square), on your left, is the city's oldest meeting place where, in the Middle Ages, everything took place; a little like Rådhusplådsen today.

Gammeltorv suffered in both fires and the town hall, which had faced

View over Strøget

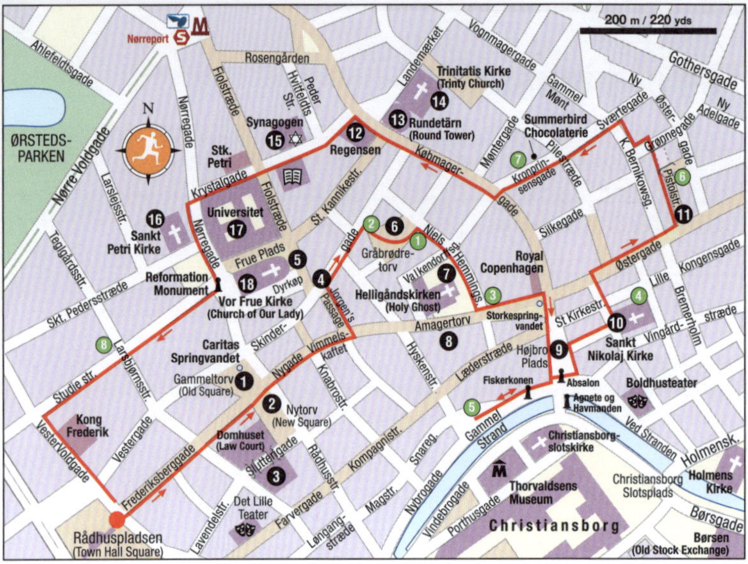

inwards on what is now the intersection with **Nytorv** ❷ (New Square), was burnt down on both occasions. Rebuilt in the same place after 1728, after the second fire it was moved to Nytorv in the hope that the space created would act as a windbreak in the event of another blaze. You can see its old outline in pale stone where the fruit-and-vegetable market usually stands.

On your left, the **Caritas Fountain** (Springvandet) is Copenhagen's oldest external water supply and is linked by pipes to a water source 6km (4 miles) away. It was a gift to the city in 1608 from Christian IV: the pregnant, lactating woman with her two children represents *Caritas* (Charity). The fountain becomes extra glitzy on important royal birthdays, when it is filled with golden apples.

The curved facade of **Stellings Hus**, designed by Arne Jacobsen (who also masterminded the *Radisson Collection Royal* hotel (see page 31), stands nearby on the corner of Skindergade.

Nytorv

On your right is where the gallows used to stand on Nytorv. The executions that took place here were well attended by bloodthirsty spectators and

The old city rooftops

provided locals with a macabre form of entertainment. Between 1720 and 1730, there were fourteen death sentences; sadly, most of them were impoverished women driven to killing their newborn babies. The last execution, of two counterfeiters, took place in 1758, though branding and whipping continued until the late 1780s. The outline of the paler stones on Nytorv shows the position of the whipping post.

On the right-hand side, you will find the classical porticoed grandeur of **Domhuset**, the third town hall, set on the former site of the Royal Orphanage, which burnt down in the fire of 1728. It was constructed between 1805 and 1815 (with a delay in 1807 when the British bombarded the city) by the architect C.F. Hansen, who was also responsible for rebuilding the cathedral, Church of Our Lady (see page 43). Domhuset was the town hall until 1905 when, owing to space issues, a new one was built on Rådhuspladsen (Town Hall Square). It is still used as Copenhagen's main Law Court (hence the large inscription above the ionic columns, 'By law shall the land be built') – the largest in Denmark. On its far side, on **Slutterigade** ❸ (Prison Street), you can see the two enclosed bridges that linked the courthouse to the prison.

Into the Latin Quarter

Carry on down Strøget until you reach the crossroads of Knabrostræde and Skoubogade – take a left for cacao heaven at **PB Chokolade** (www.pbchokolade.dk), or enjoy coffee and cake at **La Glace** (https://laglace.dk). Otherwise, continue until you see a sign for **Jorgen's Passage** ❹ on your left, an appealing arcade with some good kids' and home decor shops. Walk through to the end. Opposite is **Fiolstræde** ❺ – in the centre of the Latin Quarter around the university – with a few pretty outdoor restaurants and the back of the Church of Our Lady (Vor Frue Kirke). To experience something of the studious atmosphere, visit the excellent antiquarian and second-hand

Streets off Strøget

Although this walk takes in the major sights, don't be afraid to duck down streets shooting off the main thoroughfares that take your fancy; there are many treasures (historical and retail) around almost every corner. Unexpected finds are part of the pleasure of ambling around this area. North and south of Strøget, the streets offer more individual shopping in little one-off boutiques, record stores and second-hand shops. Roads to head for include Skindergade, Larsbjørnstræde and the three parallel streets: Vestergade, Studiestræde, Sankt Peders Stræde; and Læderstræde and Kompagnistræde, which run into each other; the latter is especially good for antiques shops.

Statue on Kobmagergade

Gråbrødretorv is a delightful café square

Fire damage

The terrible fire of 1728 raged for three days, destroying much of medieval Copenhagen. Surprisingly, when the flames died down, plans to rebuild the city in a more fireproof style were met with widespread opposition. Very few of the streets were widened – people were loath to lose their land to roadways – and although some narrow 'fire houses' were built, much of the construction was done in wood, as it was cheaper than brick.

After a second conflagration in 1795, the construction of houses in brick was enforced, and terraces had to have oblique corners to enable fire engines to navigate the area more easily, thus creating small octagonal squares all over the city. Styles changed and unadorned Neoclassical facades, without balconies, became popular.

bookshop at nos. 34–36 or grab a coffee at the library-like Paludan Café at nos. 10–12 (tel: 33 15 06 75).

Gråbrødretorv

Turn right down Skindergade (Hide Street), originally home to furriers and tanners, and walk through to **Gråbrødretorv** 6 (Grey Brothers Square), a delightful square named after the grey-clad monks who lived here from 1238 in Copenhagen's first monastery. The monks were turned out just before the Reformation in 1536, and the monastery became a hospital. Many of the houses here date from after the fire of 1728 and are known as 'fire houses', a gabled, brick-built design that was introduced in the hope that it would be more flame-proof than the medieval timbered buildings that burnt so easily.

The second fire of 1795 razed much of the rebuild – the style that followed was plainer and more classical. The square is now filled with restaurants and is a pleasant place to eat out in summer. **Yaffa**, see 1, or **Sporvejen**, see 2, are good options if you are already thinking about lunch.

Church of the Holy Ghost

Cross the square and then take a right onto Niels Hemmingsensgade. The **Church of the Holy Ghost** 7 (Helligåndskirken; Niels Hemmingsensgade 5; www.helligaandskirken.dk; free) here is on the site of a former hospice dating back as far as 1296. It was incorporated into the monastery in 1474. Much of the church, including the bells that were given by Christian IV in 1647, was destroyed in 1728. Even the coffins beneath the floor were destroyed. Surviving elements are now among some of the oldest architectural remains in Copenhagen: **Helligåndshuset**, now used for markets and exhibitions; **Christian IV's impressive main door**, made in

Colourful Skindergade houses

1630 and originally intended for the Stock Exchange (see page 81); and **Griffenfeld's Chapel**, the round burial chapel on the north side. The church was reopened in 1732. Admirers of the philosopher Søren Kirkegaard might like to note that it was here that he first saw Régine, the girl to whom he became engaged but subsequently rejected.

Amagertorv

Turn left out of the church back onto Strøget and you are almost immediately on **Amagertorv** ❽, another square punctuating the 1.5km (1-mile) length of Strøget. From here on, the shopping on Strøget becomes infinitely smarter.

Georg Jensen, Royal Copenhagen and Stork Fountain

To your left you will find two great Danish design institutions, the silversmith **Georg Jensen** (Amagertorv 4; www.georgjensen.com; free) and **Royal Copenhagen** (Amagertorv 6; www.royalcopenhagen.com; free), the handpainted porcelain manufacturer. They are housed side by side in two ornate Renaissance buildings, built for wealthy merchants.

Next door is **Illums Bolighus** (www.illumsbolighus.com), a furniture design mecca, (see page 20) and ahead of you, the **Stork Fountain** (Storkespringvandet), erected in 1894 to mark the silver wedding of Crown Prince Frederik (VIII) and his wife, Princess Louise. It's a popular meeting place, and also where newly qualified Danish midwives come for a celebratory dance!

If you are in need of a drink or a bite to eat, two good places spring to mind: the popular Gasoline Grill, see ③, or the charming **Restaurant Maven**, see ④, a short walk away at the Church of St Nicholas.

Royal Copenhagen

Royal Copenhagen, the Danish manufacturer of handmade and handpainted porcelain, was founded in 1775 by Frantz Müller, a chemist who had succeeded in mastering the difficult art of Chinese-style hard-paste porcelain. Its first designs – 'Blue Fluted', dating from 1775, based on Chinese floral motifs, and 'Blue Flower', which is a little more naturalistic and dates from 1779 – were in cobalt-blue, the only colour to withstand the high firing temperatures required. Its most ambitious design, 'Flora Danica', shows copies of botanical drawings and was originally commissioned by the king for Catherine the Great in 1790. The 1802 pieces in the range took twelve years for one artist to paint. All three designs are still in production today.

Højbro Plads

From here, turn right into **Højbro Plads** ❾, home to a dramatic

Modern glassware

The Royal Café

equestrian statue of Copenhagen's founder, Bishop Absalon. It dates from 1901 and is the work of Danish sculptors Christian Gottlieb Vilhelm Bissen, who cast the figure, and Martin Nyrop, who was responsible for the plinth. Walk down and, to your right, you will find **Gammel Strand** (Old Beach) where, from early days, fishermen used to bring in their herring catches and their wives (the 'fishwives') sold them. **Fiskerkonen**, a statue of a sturdy fishwife by Christian Svejstrup Madsen, dates from 1940 and usually stands on the corner of the steps down to the canal that still separates the Old Town from Slotsholmen (see page 80).

If you are hungry for a solid, proper, delicious lunch, one of the city's most renowned fish restaurants, **Krogs**, see 5, is located on Gammel Strand. On the other side of the canal, the porticoed building is the palace church, **Christiansborg Slotskirke** (see page 81), and to the right of that, the ochre building is the **Thorvaldsen's Museum** (see page 83). Looking ahead and to the left from the statue of Absalon, the copper roofs and twisting spire belong to the Renaissance **Børsen**, the old Stock Exchange (see page 81). The spire to the left is **Holmens Kirke**, the old navy church (see page 81).

Before turning back, cross to the middle of the bridge and look over the left side down to the water, where you will see eight figures with their hands outstretched pleadingly beneath the surface. This little-known group of statues, by sculptor Suste Bonnén, depicts part of the legend of **Agnete and the Merman**, a story in which peasant girl Agnete marries a merman and has seven sons but then fails to return after visiting her home village.

Church of St Nicholas

Walk back up towards Strøget and take a right down Lille Kirkestræde to the **Church of St Nicholas** 10 (Sankt Nikolaj Kirke; Nikolaj Plads 10; www.nikolajkunsthal.dk; charge, free Wed), named after the patron saint of sailors – an apt sponsor in a seaboard town. The mother church of the Reformation in 1536, it survived the 1728 fire, but was not so lucky in 1795 when everything but the tower was razed to the ground. Rebuilt in rather imposing red brick in the early twentieth century, it is now an exhibition hall for modern art.

On to Købmagergade

Head over Store Kirkestraede back onto Strøget. Turn right down to Kristen Bernikows Gade and cross the road. To your right you will see the back of Magasin du Nord (see page 46) and a small flower market. Continue until you reach a signposted archway for **Pistolstræde** 11. Walk to the end, past various smart shops, until you reach the little courtyard with **L'Alsace**, see 6,which has hosted Pope John Paul II and Elton

Statue of Bishop Absalon

John, no less. Here, you will see the timbered backs of seventeenth-century houses; unusual in an Old Town that has succumbed to two major fires.

Walk through to Grønnegade, a pretty street (look at the houses to your right) and turn left, then right back onto Kristen Bernikows Gade. Take the first left onto Sværtergade: the little yellow building on the right, constructed immediately after the first fire, is the smallest house in the old town. One block further, Sværtergade turns into Kronprinsensgade, one of Copenhagen's poshest shopping streets (even if it does have a 7/11 on the corner). **Summerbird Chocolaterie** (Kronprinsensgade 11; https://summerbird.dk), another well-known chocolate-maker, can be found along here, as can Copenhagen's oldest teashop, **A.C. Perch Thehandel**, see 7, at No. 5.

At the end, turn right onto Købmagergade. Opposite you is the former site of the **Post & Tele Museum** (now being rebuilt in Østerbro in the north of the city) and further down on your right, the **Round Tower**; **Trinity Church** next to it; and, opposite, **Regensen** 12, a seventeenth-century student hall of residence, which is still in use.

Round Tower

Continue down Købmagergade until you see the **Round Tower** (Rundetårn) 13 (Kobmagergade 52a; www.rundetaarn.dk; free), the round red-brick tower on your right. This unusual edifice is a seventeenth-century observatory, the oldest in Europe, and was used by astronomers at the University of Copenhagen until 1861. It was the tallest building in Copenhagen when Christian IV had it built, and is thought to be mentioned in H.C. Andersen's fairytale of the *Soldier and the Tinder Box*, where a dog is described as having 'eyes as big as a tower'. Andersen knew this tower well and, as an observatory, it was literally an 'eye' on the heavens.

Inside, a wide cobbled ramp spirals up through the tower, designed for a horse and cart to use (the only practical way of taking heavy equipment all the way to the top). In 1716, Tsar Peter of Russia himself galloped his horse to the top of the 209-metre (686ft) ramp inside the Round Tower, followed more sedately by his wife in a carriage. Now, a unicycle race to the top and back is hosted every year, usually held in May. There is also an art gallery, formerly the university library, about half-way up.

Trinity Church

Next door, **Trinity Church** 14 (Trinitatis Kirke; Købmagergade 52a/ Landemærket 12; www.trinitatiskirke.dk; free) was commissioned as the university church by Christian IV, and finished in 1657 under Frederik III.

Although the Round Tower survived the blaze of 1728, the church suffered.

Folk musicians

The Round Tower

Its roof, and the university library that lay beneath it, were charred to a crisp and the interiors damaged. But it was quickly restored by 1731 and is now a lovely white-and-gold Rococo affair with a splendid Baroque altarpiece, a three-faced Rococo clock, a vaulted roof picked out in gold, galleries running down both side walls and a fabulous gold- and silver-coloured organ. If it is open, it is worth a visit; otherwise, look down the nave through a glass panel as you head up the Round Tower.

Krystalgade

Continue and turn left up Krystalgade, the spire of the Church of Our Lady (Vor Frue Kirke) in view. The large red-brick building set behind grey railings a little way up on your right is Copenhagen's **Grand Synagogue** ⓯ (Synagogen; usually closed to the public except pre-arranged bookings, see https://mosaiske.dk). The centre for Judaism in Denmark, it dates from 1883 and, amazingly, survived the Nazi occupation. Its interior is notable for Egyptian-influenced elements. Its sacred Torah scrolls were hidden in Trinity Church during World War II.

Cross over Filostræde. The back of the university building is on your left – look for the book stacks through the windows – and the **1 Hotel Copenhagen** (www.1hotels.com/copenhagen), where you can settle down for an early evening cocktail, is a little further up.

Nørregade

At the end of the street, take a left onto Nørregade. On your right is the **Church of St Peter** ⓰.

Church of St Peter

The first Church of St Peter (Sankt Petri Kirke; Larslejsstæde 11) was built here in around 1200 in the Romanesque style. It burnt down and was replaced, *c.*1450, with a Gothic structure, minus the transepts, which were added in the seventeenth century.

During the Reformation, the church was deconsecrated and turned into a canon foundry, but in 1585 it was reinstated and given to the German-speaking population by Frederik II. German was the main language spoken by the court and, as a result, Sankt Petri became an important intellectual, economic and political meeting place.

The fire of 1728 destroyed its interior, and new decoration, including the Baroque main entrance (1730s) and the copper-clad spire (1757), were introduced. Its vaulted sepulchral chapel (1681–83), which has some impressive statuary, is the resting place of the royal architect Nicolai Eigtved (1701–54), who designed the church spire; and possibly of the German doctor Johann Struensee (1737–72), who stepped into the king's shoes and ruled Denmark for over a year (see page 84).

The main post office building

The university

On your left, as you walk towards the Church of Our Lady, there is a square. The building facing the side of the church is the **university** ⓱ (*universitet*). There has been a university in Copenhagen since 1479 and it currently educates around 37,000 students. It was located on the corner of Nørregade and Studiestræde until just after the Reformation in 1536, when it was moved across the street to the vacated Bishops Palace.

The fires of 1728 and 1795 and the British Navy bombardment in 1807 made short work of any ancient buildings and the current one dates from the nineteenth century. The portrait busts are of illustrious professors.

Church of Our Lady

Copenhagen's cathedral, the **Church of Our Lady** ⓲ (Vor Frue Kirke; Nørregade, Vor Frue Plads; www.domkirken.dk; free) is the latest in a long line of church buildings, dating back to 1209, to stand on this spot. Fires destroyed two of the earlier churches, and the current building was designed to replace the one destroyed by the British bombardment of 1807, when the navy used the church spire as a target. The brainchild of C.F. Hansen, it dates from 1829: only the tower and the walls of the side aisles remain of the medieval building. The front door is guarded by towering statues of **King David** and **Moses**, while the interior is noteworthy for its reliefs and imposing marble statues by Bertel Thorvaldsen (see page 83), dating from 1839. These include **Christ and the 12 Apostles** (with Judas replaced by St Paul) on the altar and along the side walls; and the beautiful angel holding a shell, which serves as the cathedral's font. Two of its four bells have claims to fame: one, dating to 1490, is the oldest in the country; while 'Stormklokken' is the heaviest bell in Denmark, weighing a hefty four tons.

Royal weddings

When Crown Prince Frederik married Australian commoner Mary Donaldson in 2004, walking her down the aisle of the Church of Our Lady (Vor Frue Kirke), he was following in the footsteps of some of his forebears: Queen Margrethe I who, at the age of nine, married the Norwegian king Haakan in 1363; and Christian I who married his queen, Dorothea, here in 1449. The Danish monarchy holds the record for unbroken succession from the Viking chief Gorm the Old, father of Harald Bluetooth, who died in c.958, of fifty kings (predominantly named Frederik or Christian) and two queens, both Margrethe – the second celebrated her Ruby Jubliee (forty years on the throne) in 2012.

The Caritas Fountain

The University of Copenhagen

Food and drink

1 Yaffa
Gråbrødretorv 11; http://yaffa.dk; €€
This easy-going spot specialises in comforting Mediterranean classics, with falafel, grilled octopus and fattoush salads bringing some sun to the grey Copenhagen skies.

2 Sporvejen
Grabrødretorv 17; www.sporvejen.dk; €
Cheap and cheerful fare (omelettes, burgers and so on) in an old Copenhagen tram. Sit out on the square in summer.

3 Gasoline Grill
Østergade 59; www.gasolinegrill.com; €
Now a small local chain, this is the original location of the ever-popular hamburger joint – inside a disused petrol station. Good fun, and a reassuringly small menu of classic burgers.

4 Restaurant Maven
Nikolaj Plads 12;
www.restaurantmaven.dk; €€
This acclaimed bistro serves well-presented French-Danish food in a romantic setting inside a former church.

5 Krogs
Gammel Strand 38; www.krogs.dk; €€€€
Booking is essential if you wish to dine at Copenhagen's oldest fish restaurant. The four-course evening menu starts at 595dkk (€80).

6 L'Alsace
Ny Østergade 9; www.alsace.dk; €€€€
Gourmet food from France, specialising in Alsace. The three-course lunch menu is good value.

7 A.C. Perch Thehandel
Kronprinsessgade 5;
www.perchstearoom.dk; €€
This teashop has barely changed since 1835, and it offers an astonishing variety of blends. There's also a deliciously tea-centric café on the first floor.

8 The Living Room
Larsbjørnsstræde 17;
http://thelivingroom.dk; €
This two-floor café-bar serves a wide range of coffees as well as a selection of cocktails. A mix between traditional Danish home comforts and Moroccan decor.

Outside the cathedral, the **monument** on Bispetorvet commemorates the 400th anniversary of the Reformation. Cross the square and head down Studiestræde opposite the Church of Our Lady, past **The Living Room**, see 8. Take a left at the next junction and a short walk will bring you back to Rådhuspladsen.

Inside the Church of Our Lady

WALK 3
The harbour area

This walk is a short but colourful one, starting in Kongens Nytorv (King's New Square), the height of seventeenth-century aristocratic elegance, and leading down to Nyhavn. Once known for its brothels and seedy taverns, today the harbour is a popular outdoor area peppered with attractive restaurants and bars.

DISTANCE: 1km (0.5 miles)
TIME: 1hr (plus boat trip 1hr)
START: *Hôtel d'Angleterre*
END: Nyhavn
POINTS TO NOTE: If you don't take a harbour cruise, this is a nice walk to do at the end of the day, ending on Nyhavn for a drink or dinner. If you walk up one of the side streets onto Sankt Annae Plads, it connects easily with the walk of the Royal District (see page 49).

In the Middle Ages, Kongens Nytorv, an elegant square that now seems integral to Copenhagen, was outside the city walls and quite a distance from the banks of the Sound. It began to develop under Frederik III (1648–70). Between 1671 and 1673, his son Christian V (1670–99) commissioned a canal (now called Nyhavn, or 'New Harbour') to be dug from the Sound to the square so that merchant ships could sail inland and unload their cargo more easily. He also ordered landowners with property bordering on the square to build grand mansions or to sell their land to someone who would.

Kongens Nytorv

Standing at the bottom of **Strøget** (see page 37), you face Kongens Nytorv with Nyhavn (out of sight) lying on the far side of the square. The metro station is currently being extended to make Kongens Nytorv an interchange for the new Cityringen metro line and, during the pre-construction phase, archaeologists discovered the East Gate of the eleventh-century city here. To your left, at the corner of the square, is Copenhagen's swankiest hotel, the **Hôtel d'Angleterre** (www.dangleterre.com); to your right is **Magasin du Nord** (www.magasin.dk), the city's oldest department store.

Hôtel d'Angleterre

The **Hôtel d'Angleterre** ❶ has seen more than its fair share of rich and famous visitors since opening its

The imposing Hôtel d'Angleterre

doors in 1755. The guestlist is an illustrious roll call of big-name stars: H.C. Andersen, Grace Kelly, Winston Churchill, Margaret Thatcher, Bill Clinton, Woody Allen, Pierce Brosnan and Madonna. When Michael Jackson stayed in the 1980s, he was so enthralled by some of its furnishings that he wanted to buy them; when politely told they were not for sale, he offered to buy the entire hotel instead. Oddly enough, they declined.

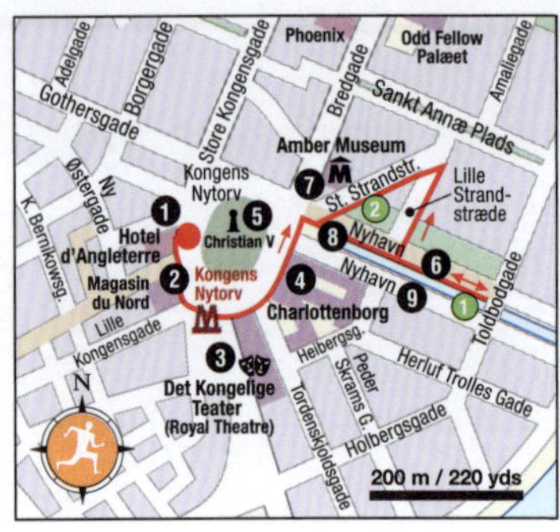

Magasin du Nord

Originally a hotel, the **Magasin du Nord** ❷ dates from the nineteenth century. At Vingårdstræde 6 is an attic room where Hans Christian Andersen lived while he was studying for his exams in 1827. The department store is also a good stop for a coffee or bite to eat (though you definitely pay for the location).

The Royal Theatre and Kunsthal Charlottenborg

The **Royal Theatre** ❸ (Det Kongelige Teater; see page 22) stands opposite the Magasin du Nord on the south side of the square. There has been a theatre here since 1748; the present classically inspired incarnation was built in the 1870s. It has been somewhat eclipsed by the strikingly modern Royal Danish Playhouse (see page 22). Catch a glimpse of the 1930s mosaic ceiling from August Bournonvilles Passage, to the side of the theatre.

East of the theatre, **Kunsthal Charlottenborg** ❹ (www.kunsthalcharlottenborg.dk; charge) was built in the seventeenth century as a palatial residence for Frederik III's illegitimate son, Ulrik. Less than a century later, it became the Royal Danish Academy of Fine Arts, where painters, sculptors and architects learned their trade. It is now used for contemporary art exhibitions.

Equestrian statue of Christian V

Look to the centre of the square, where you will see a large **equestrian statue of Christian V** ❺ dressed as a Roman emperor, riding over the fallen figure of Envy. The king is surrounded by Queen Artemisia, Alexander the Great, the goddess Pallas Athene and Hercules. Carved by the French sculptor and stonemason Abraham César Lamoureux, it was the first equestrian statue in Scandinavia and was originally made of gilded lead because bronze castings of this size were not possible at the time.

Kunsthal Charlottenborg exhibit

It has been repaired many times and, in 1946, was recast in bronze. The original can now be found in Christian IV's Brewery (Bryghus; see page 85).

Nyhavn

At the bottom of Kongens Nytorv, the 'New Harbour', or **Nyhavn** ❻, is lined with pastel-coloured merchants' houses that date from when the canal was constructed. Their warehouses stood at the end; a couple still survive and are now smart boutique hotels, *The Admiral* and *71 Nyhavn* (see page 109).

With its attractive historical ships at anchor, Nyhavn is not just of interest for its seventeenth- and eighteenth-century maritime past. From the 1880s, it was also the gateway to a new life in the US, since it was here that you bought your ticket from one of the many shipping offices that sprang up. A new start for many, although not for the fourteen unfortunates who set sail to join the *Titanic*'s maiden voyage in 1912, of whom only two survived.

The entrance to Nyhavn is heralded by a large **anchor**, honouring 1600 Danish sailors who lost their lives in World War II. To the left as you face the Sound, the **Amber Museum** ❼ (Kongens Nytorv 2; www.houseofamber.com) showcases Denmark's national gemstone. When you learn that most amber deposits weigh 10g (0.5oz) or less each, you will understand the wonder of the chunk weighing a record-breaking 8.8kg (19lbs 6oz) that is on display here.

Hans Christian Andersen spent around 22 years lodging at various addresses in Nyhavn, because it was close to the Royal Theatre, which he loved. He wrote his first fairy tales, including *The Tinder Box* and *The Princess and the Pea*, at **No. 20** (then 289) – such a cold house that, in winter, his landlady's children poured water on the floor to make ice slides. He also lived for twenty years at **No. 67** and ended his days at **No. 18**.

Nyhavn's north side

The sunny side of the canal is a popular restaurant area; sit inside or out (blankets and heaters are provided in winter), but grab a seat while you can, as it is almost always busy. The restaurants are all in old buildings and have names such as Skipperkroen (the Skipper's Inn), **Cap Horn**, see ①, or La Sirène (the Siren); they are linked to the lives and travels of the sailors who used to saunter along here looking for women, drink and a bed.

Side streets

The side streets off Nyhavn are well worth exploration and, like the harbour itself, have come up in the world. The first turning on your left takes you up **Store Strandstræde** (Big Beach Street), the only remnant of its seafaring past is a tattoo parlour that claims to have been on the site since the sixteenth century. There's a nice little restaurant along here called **Zeleste**, see ②.

Picturesque Nyhavn

The Royal Theatre

Food and drink

1 Cap Horn
Nyhavn 21; www.caphorn.dk; €€
Nyhavn eateries are more about people-watching than food, but this appealing place serves good grub too, including lamb, deer and duck dishes, and some lighter fish mains.

2 Zeleste
Store Strandstraede 6; https://zeleste.dk; €€
Pretty whitewashed restaurant with a cobbled courtyard and a hearty, regularly changing menu. Great brunches. Book to avoid disappointment.

Continue along and at the end turn right, back on yourself, down **Lille Strandstræde** (Little Beach Street), also dotted with small galleries and clothes shops. Carry on to the end and you will find yourself back on Nyhavn.

Boat trips round the harbour

Seeing the city from the water is a great way to understand the layout. If you want to take a boat trip, you will find the **Strömma** (Gray Line; www.stromma.dk) tour boats 8 at the top of Nyhavn near the anchor, and the **Netto Bådene** (www.havnerundfart.dk) boats 9 further along the south side of the canal. The blue-and-yellow local transport boats also call at the jetty at the end of Nyhavn.

The usual route passes by the Royal Danish Playhouse (see page 22); the **Opera House** (see page 90); and **Langelinie**, **Kastellet** and ***The Little Mermaid*** (see page 53). Some tours venture further out to **Trekroner**, an eighteenth-century fort used once in 1801 against the British, before turning back to sail past **Christianshavn** (see page 86), down the **Frederiksberg Kanal**, then past **Slotsholmen** (see page 80) and the royal palace, the **Bryghus**, the **Black Diamond** and **Holmens Kirke**, and back to Nyhavn.

View of the harbour

WALK 4
The royal district

This walk takes you through Copenhagen's grandest quarter, Frederiksstaden, and then along the banks of the Sound. Once a heaving commercial and naval area, its quiet streets are now frequented by tourists and locals, including the royal family, who live at Amalienborg palace at its heart.

DISTANCE: 4km (2.5 miles)
TIME: A half-day
START: Sankt Annæ Plads
END: Kongens Nytorv
POINTS TO NOTE: Most of the food options are towards the end of the walk near Bredgade, which makes this a good choice for a morning walk. Alternatively, have a picnic by the Sound or in Kastellet.

In 1749, Frederik V laid the foundation stone for his building project, Frederiksstad, a grand court district adorned with a large and beautiful church rivalling almost anything else in Europe. He was an absolute monarch, belonging to the 300-year-old Oldenburg dynasty, and wanted to create something startling – and he did. He even got his wealthy subjects to pay for it. The rococo palaces of the Amalienborg were designed for four aristocratic families in the 1750s by royal architect Nicolai Eigtved. Several decades later, the royal family moved in, and Amalienborg is still their winter home.

Start at **Sankt Annæ Plads** ❶, a tree-lined boulevard created during the construction of Frederiksstaden, when a former canal was filled in. A large **equestrian statue of Christian X** (1912–47) presides over the top end of the 'square', while the harbour end is dominated by the Royal Danish Playhouse (see page 22). Close to the statue is the **Garrison's Church** ❷ (Garnisons Kirke; www.garnisonskirken.dk; free) and its graveyard, built to replace the castle chapel that burned down in 1689. Copenhagen's garrison attended church here from 1706. The plain white interior is composed of unusual two-storey galleries, with a dramatic black altarpiece (1724) providing the main focus of attention.

Amalienborg

From here, cross the square and turn left up **Amaliegade**. Before he became a 'Prince of Denmark' in 1852, at the

Sankt Annæ Plads at dusk

age of 34, Christian IX lived with his family in a yellow townhouse at Amaliegade 18, where four of his children were born. Today it is still an exclusive street studded with embassies and some of the most elegant and expensive buildings in the city. If you need a bite to eat check out **Restaurant Amalie**, see 1, or the equally popular **Café Toldboden**, see 2. Duck through the arch that leads into the grandest part of Frederiksstad, flanked by the four palaces of **Amalienborg** 3.

The palaces

Amalienborg was built on the site of a previous palace which burned down in a horrific fire: during a theatrical performance on 19 April 1689 for Christian V's birthday, part of the stage caught alight and 180 people died in the blaze.

In 1794, the royal family moved in after a fire at Slotsholmen (see page 80), and liked their new home so much that the king purchased all four buildings. They have

Amalienborg Castle

lived here ever since, members often occupying each palace at different times.

As you stand in the centre of the octagonal 'square' looking back at the colonnade, to your right is **Christian VII's palace** ❹ (Christian VII's Palæ; charge; book at www.kongernessamling.dk), one of the first to be finished before Eigtved died in 1754. This was originally the sumptuous home of Lord High Steward Adam Gottlob Moltke and the most expensive of the four; it is widely considered to shelter Denmark's best rococo interior. Christian VII, who suffered from mental illness for much of his reign, lived here from December 1794 until his death in 1808. The queen now uses it to welcome foreign dignitaries.

On the left of the colonnade, which connects the two palaces, you'll find **Christian IX's Palace** ❺ (Christian IX's Palæ), which is home to Queen Margrethe and Prince Henrik, and was originally known as Schack's Palace. Crown Prince Frederik VI and his wife Marie were the first royals to move in and lived here for over forty years. Frederik was Regent and ruled for his father between 1784 and 1808. Even so, he often needed his father's signature for affairs of state, so he had the colonnade built between the two palaces, with a corridor running through it for easy access.

Turn your back on these palaces and to your left is **Christian VIII's Palace** ❻ (Christian VIII's Palæ), originally called the Levetzau Palace. Part of the palace is open all year as a **museum** to the Glücksberg dynasty (www.kongernessamling.dk; charge) – the entrance is by Frederiksgade. Here, you can see the chintzy drawing room of Queen Louise and the studies of Frederik VIII, Frederik IX, Christian IX and Christian X, which have all been moved from other parts of Amalienborg.

On your right is **Frederik VIII's Palace** ❼ (Frederik VIII's Palæ), with a clock on its facade, which is the home of King Frederik X and Queen Mary of Denmark.

Christian IX

Christian IX (1863–1906), for whom one of the Amalienborg palaces is named, came to be known as the 'father-in-law of Europe' because his six children married into the royal families of Sweden, Britain, Russia, Germany and France. A nephew of the childless Frederik VII (1848–63), he was the first king since Christian I (1448–81) not to succeed his father or grandfather, and, although a choice favoured by the Danes, he was not the nearest legal heir. Christian improved his claim by marrying Louise of Hesse, who was more closely related on the female side. His daughter Alexandra married King Edward VII of Britain (who reigned between 1901 and 1910), son of Queen Victoria.

Standing guard

Christian VIII's Palace

In the centre of the square is an equestrian statue of **Frederik V**, dressed as a Roman emperor. Sculptor Jacques Saly took over twenty years to complete the monument owing, allegedly, to his commitment to having fun. The final price tag was said to have been higher than the cost of the palace itself. The statue here is a copy: the original, unveiled in 1771 with a 21-gun salute, is on display in the Lapidarium on Slotsholmen (see page 85).

Amalienborg is guarded by the Royal Life Guards. When the king is in residence, they are replaced at noon by the guards from Rosenborg Palace.

The Marble Church

If you stand with your back to the equestrian statue, you will see the spectacular **Marble Church** ❽ (Marmorkirken; Frederiksgade 4; www.marmorkirken.dk; free) or, more properly, 'Frederikskirke' (after the monarch). It was designed as a very important part of the Frederiksstad by Nicolai Eigtved in 1740; yet, thirty years on, it remained unfinished and funds had run out. It languished in ruins for over a century when help came in the guise of an industrialist, Carl Frederik Tietgen, and it was inaugurated in 1894. A massive dome stands on twelve pillars and is covered in paintings of the twelve apostles, light flooding in from twelve skylights. At 31 metres (101ft) in diameter, the **dome** is second only in size to that of St Peter's in Rome, which measures 42 metres (137ft). You can scale the summit at 1pm and 3pm (daily mid-June to August, Saturday and Sunday rest of year; charge) for wonderful views.

Outside, at ground level, there are fourteen Danish 'Fathers of the Church' and, higher up, eighteen figures of prophets, apostles and figures from Church history, finishing with Martin Luther.

Alexander Nevsky Church

Coming out of the church, look left up Bredgade – an exclusive street full of antique shops and auction houses – to glimpse the golden onion domes of **Alexander Nevsky Church** ❾ (Alexandr Nevsky Kirke; Bredgade 53; free), a Russian orthodox church, built in 1883 as a gift from Tsar Alexander III to mark his marriage to Princess Marie Dagmar.

Walk back to Amalienborg and through the square to the waterside, where you will find **Amalie Haven** ❿, a pretty park directly across from the **Opera House** (see page 90).

Along the harbour

Walk along the harbourside, chimneys and windmills visible in the distance, until you reach a copy of Michelangelo's statue of *David*. This heralds the **Royal Cast Collection** ⓫ (Den Kongelige Afstøbningssamling; Vestindisk Pakhus, Toldbodgade 40; open for special events only). Set in an

Gefionspringvandet

eighteenth-century warehouse, replicas of over two thousand famous statues chart the history of sculpture from Ancient Egypt and antiquity onwards.

Continue for another 250 metres/yds along the harbourside until you see the green-topped pavilions on the quayside. It is from here that the royal family take a tender when boarding their yacht *Dannebrog*. Turn left onto **Esplanaden**, which used to be a busy thoroughfare between the docks and **Nyboder**, Christian IV's naval housing estate built in 1631. Turning right along Churchillparken, the fenced-off area on your immediate left was the site of the **Frihedsmuseet** (Resistance Museum), dedicated to exploring the German Occupation between 1940 and 1945. The museum suffered a terrible fire in 2013, and the building was torn down. A new museum was built from scratch, and opened to the public in 2019.

Further along Churchillparken are the nineteenth-century mock-Gothic English **Church of St Albans** and the fountain **Gefionspringvandet** (inaugurated in 1909). Commissioned by Carl Jacobsen, the dramatic **statue** ⓬ above the tiers of water shows the goddess Gefion driving a plough and four oxen at great speed. She had tricked the Swedish king, who did not know her identity, into letting her have as much land as she could plough in one night, so she transformed her four giant sons and cultivated enough land to create the island of Sjælland (Zealand).

Marie Dagmar

Marie Dagmar, the second daughter of Christian IX, married the future Tsar Alexander III in St Petersburg in 1866. She had, in fact, been betrothed to Alexander's brother, Nicholas, in 1864 but he had died suddenly of tuberculous meningitis a few months after their engagement. She became known as Maria Feodorovna and had four sons and two daughters, including Tsar Nicholas II and the Grand Duke Michael who were both murdered during the Russian Revolution in 1918. She escaped to London in 1919 and eventually returned to Denmark where she died in 1928. Her funeral was held at Alexander Nevsky Church, and she was buried in Roskilde Cathedral. In 2005, her remains were returned to St Petersburg, as she had wished, to be buried beside her husband.

Towards the Little Mermaid

Cross over the bridge behind the Gefion fountain back to the waterside. The quayside is studded with statues: the first on your left is of Frederik IX (1947–72), Queen Margrethe's father; a little further on is a bronze bust of one Princess Marie, who died young, hence the mourning mother and child at the base of the sculpture.

Continue on and you will reach **The Little Mermaid** ⓭ (Lille Havfrue, 1913), commissioned by the

Marble Church dome

Alexandr Nevsky Church

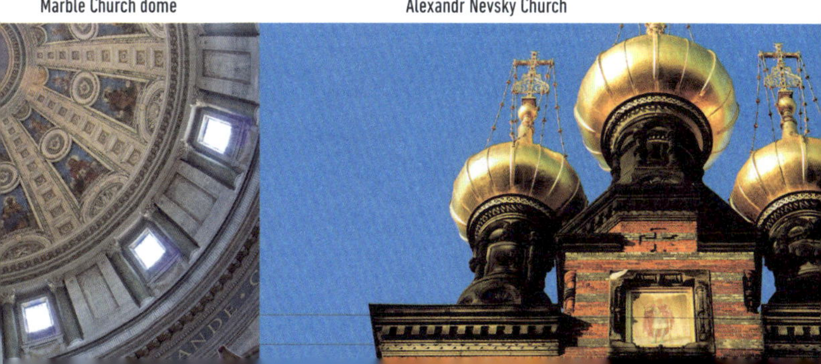

Carlsberg Foundation in 1909. Edvard Eriksen's small, gentle figure staring out to sea was modelled on his wife Eline. Now, controversial artist Bjørn Nørgaard has produced *The Genetically Modified Little Mermaid* (2008), a grotesque sculpture that poses on a similar rock 400 metres (1312ft) from the long-suffering original.

This walk now turns back towards the city centre; but if you are peckish, stroll a little further beyond the marina to **Tio Marios**, see 3, a popular lunch spot for ferry passengers and local businesspeople. If you're feeling flush, the Langelinie Outlet Stores are on the other side of the two basins, on the quayside.

Kastellet

Follow Langelinie round, cross the bridge, with the marina on your right, and head down the steps to **Kastellet** 14, Copenhagen's star-shaped fort, dating from 1662. Over 350 years later, it is still in use by the military. Nonetheless, it is a delightfully peaceful enclave, with seventeenth- and eighteenth-century buildings. There's a charming **windmill** and the grassy ramparts (free) are pleasant to wander around.

Towards Nyboder

Walk through Kastellet and you will come back onto Esplanaden. Just opposite, pause for a well-earned coffee at **Kafferiet**, see 4, a small coffee shop in a pale-blue, eighteenth-century townhouse. If you are looking for something more substantial, turn left up Esplanaden towards the harbour until you reach **Lumskebugten**, see 5.

If you want to take a look at **Nyboder** 15, carry on down Esplanaden, away from the harbour, until you reach the grid of ochre-coloured houses. The area's distinctive homes were built by Christian IV in response to a desperate housing shortage for navy personnel. Its inhabitants received free housing and education but, in return, all boys went to sea for sixteen to twenty years of compulsory service. Naval law applied to the women and children as well as the men.

Otherwise, take the first left down Bredgade, where you will find **Café Petersborg**, see 6; or the second left onto Store Kongensgade for something hearty and simple at **Dandelion Burger**, see 7.

Designmuseum Danmark

Set in Frederiksstad's former hospital (1754–1910), the **Designmuseum Danmark** 16 (Bredgade 68; www.designmuseum.dk; charge) is an interesting journey through the history of household design. From Harley-Davidsons to cardboard chairs, medieval handicrafts to rococo furniture, you will be hard pushed not to find something appealing, although most of the information is in Danish. It has a pretty garden and an indoor café with good cakes.

The church in Kastellet

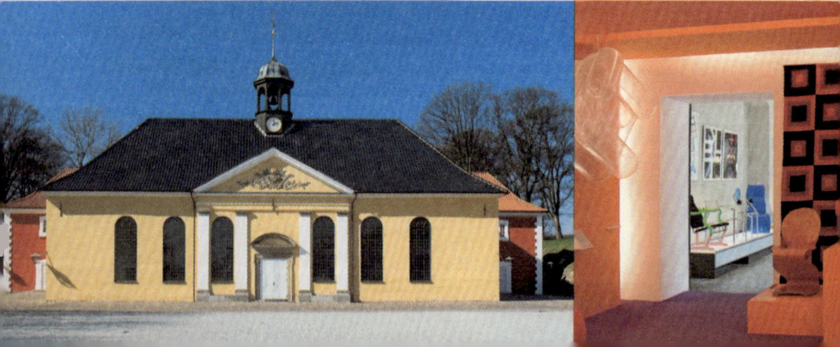

Food and drink

1 Restaurant Amalie
Amaliegade 11;
http://restaurantamalie.dk; €€
This wood-panelled, candlelit lunch spot serves up delicious Danish *smørrebrød*. Good value for the quality.

2 Cafe Toldboden
Amaliegade 41;
www.cafetoldboden.dk; €€€
Join the local suits who call by for their lunchtime *smørrebrød* in this eighteenth-century townhouse. Book to be sure of a seat.

3 Tio Marios
Amerika Pl. 4; http://tiomarios.dk; €€
Stop on the west basin for a hearty lunch of pizza, pasta or a burger or wrap.

4 Kafferiet
Esplanaden 44; http://kafferiet.dk; €
Enjoy excellent double-roast coffee at this quirky café in a duck-egg-blue townhouse, illuminated by home-made lamps.

5 Lumskebugten
Esplanaden 21;
www.lumskebugten.dk; €€
Charming, airy restaurant in a former sailors' tavern given to leisurely meals.

6 Café Petersborg
Bredgade 76;
www.cafe-petersborg.dk; €€
Excellent Danish café-restaurant in the beamed basement of a house dating from 1746. Pick between a *smørrebrød* or a full meal.

7 Dandelion Burger
Store Kongensgade 70;
www.dandelionburger.com; €
Beloved local spot for a juicy burger, with high-quality patties boosted with bone marrow and aged organic cheddar.

8 Alida Marstrand
Bredgade 14; www.alidamarstrand.dk; €€
This small chocolatier opened in 1930, with confectionery recipes gleaned from the Tzar's court, and has since stood the test of time.

The Medical Museum

The **Medical Museum** 17 (Medicinsk Museion; Bredgade 62; www.museion.ku.dk; charge) is next door. Not for the squeamish, but a fascinating collection of the peculiarities and horrors of medicine in a bygone age.

Now, head south towards Kongens Nytorv. To finish this walking tour on an indulgent note, pop by **Alida Marstrand**, see 8, one of Copenhagen's superior purveyors of handmade chocolates and traditional marzipan pigs.

Designmuseum Danmark

Ochre-coloured houses in Nyboder

WALK 5
Around Rosenborg

Rosenborg Slot seems remarkable not just for its beauty but also its position bang in the middle of Copenhagen, surrounded by elegant townhouses, the botanical gardens and a couple of lovely art galleries.

DISTANCE: 2km (1.5 miles)
TIME: A half-/full day
START: David Collection
END: Hirschsprung Collection
POINTS TO NOTE: If you find yourself short on time, visit Rosenborg Palace and the National Gallery of Art (see page 62) and just walk through the King's Gardens and the botanical gardens. The latter make for a welcoming break if you have had your dose of historical artefacts and paintings.

The Dutch Renaissance-style castle Rosenborg is a real highlight of the city. However, when the architect-king Christian IV built it in 1606, it actually stood outside Copenhagen, in the countryside beyond the northeastern ramparts. Christiansborg was a crumbling mess at the time, and the royal residence of Frederiksborg lay an inconvenient 35km (22 miles) away, so it made sense to have a palace closer to the city.

Rosenborg was built in several stages (see page 59); by 1624, it was much as it is today. It is still surrounded by the pretty **King's Gardens** (Kongens Have), a welcome green area, and extremely popular with Copenhageners. Around three million people stroll, sunbathe and picnic here each year. The city council has invested heavily in the parks and museums around the castle, and has introduced the Parkmuseerne combined ticket (www.kongernessamling.dk), which gives visitors cheaper entry to the castle, the Cinematheque and three museums: the Hirschsprung Collection, the National Gallery of Denmark and the Natural History Museum.

The most impressive way to approach Rosenborg is through the gardens from the Kronprinsessegade gate. However, before you enter, take half an hour or so in the **David Collection** ❶ (Davids Samling; Kronprinsessegade 30–32; www.davidmus.dk; free), a fine curation of European fine arts and Islamic and Eastern art from the seventh to the nineteenth centuries.

The collection is housed in an old townhouse – worth a visit in

Ornately tiled stove in the David Collection

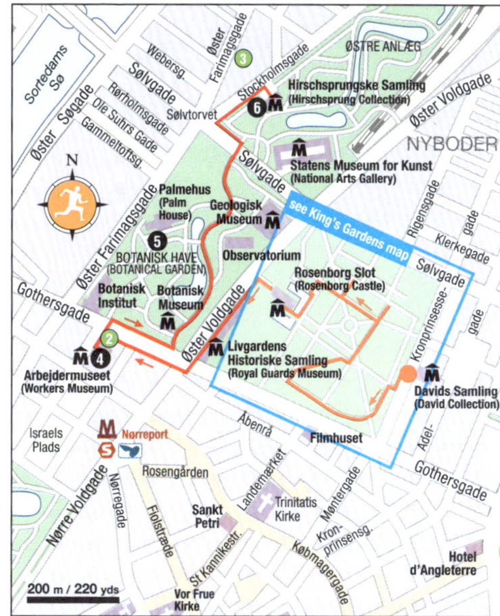

itself – on a street that, until the fire of 1795, was part of the King's Gardens. After the fire, King Frederik VI donated a strip of land to the city and a long line of Neoclassical houses was built. The sale of these financed rebuilding in the Old Town. At the same time, twelve dinky little shop-pavilions were created along the park's edge, and are still in use today.

King's Gardens

From the entrance to the **King's Gardens** ❷ (Kongens Have; free), you will see the best view of the turreted romantic castle, straight down the crocus lawn (finest in spring), lined with marble spheres dating from 1674. The fortress sits on its own island within the gardens, and is accessed by the Grønnebro (Green Bridge) over the moat.

In their early days, the gardens provided the palace with fish from three ponds and fresh produce from fruit orchards and vegetable gardens. Even when the castle became state property in 1849, Rosenborg continued to furnish the royal kitchen until 1909.

Wander at will or follow our route below to see the gardens' main attractions before visiting the castle.

Krumspringet

Turn left at the Kronprinsessegade entrance and walk around the edge of the park until you reach the second path on your right. Turn right and right again to visit the **Krumspringet** Ⓐ, a maze of narrow paths arranged in a symmetrical pattern. This one is modern, but old garden plans show that there was a maze here back in the seventeenth

Rosenborg Slot and the King's Gardens

century. The name comes from the Danish for 'dodge' because people could avoid unwanted meetings by nipping out of the way down one of its labyrinthine paths. Walk to the centre and then out again, by the next path on the right, which will bring you to the **crocus lawn** B, a truly spectacular sight in spring.

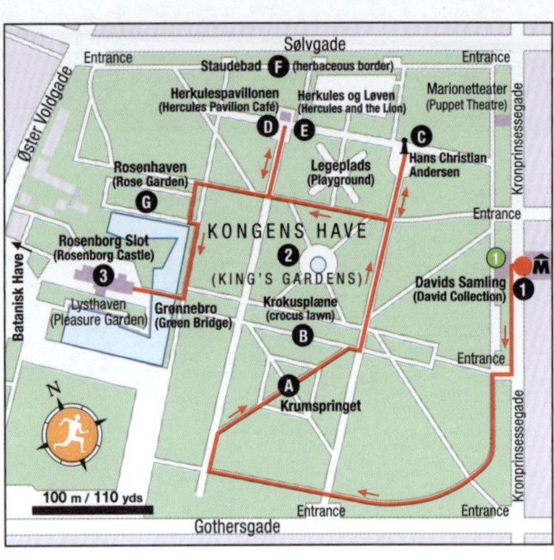

Hans Christian Andersen

With the castle on your left, head on down the Allé. For a civilised coffee break, branch off diagonally for the **Orangeriet**, see 1. Otherwise, continue straight on the **statue of Hans Christian Andersen** C, which was designed and cast during Andersen's lifetime and he had input in to how he was portrayed. The sculptor, August Saaybe, was expecting to include children listening to the storyteller – but Andersen objected, saying that he hated having anyone sitting or standing close to him when he read; and that his fairy tales were intended as much for adults as for children. The monument was eventually unveiled in 1880, after Andersen's death. Attractive reliefs depicting his stories adorn the plinth.

Hercules Pavilion and statue

Turn back and take the first right. Head past a playground and then turn right to come face to face with the **Hercules Pavilion** D and a modern **statue of Hercules and the Lion** E performing the first of his Twelve Labours: strangling the Nemean Lion with his bare hands in an attempt to atone for the murder of his three children. The original marble, bought by Frederik IV in 1709 on a trip to Italy, crumbled away: this is a modern copy.

The pavilion (now a café), first known as the 'Blue Arbour', was altered by Christian V so that his family could eat without the servants being present. Beyond the pavilion, the twentieth-century **herbaceous border** F unfurls over 250 metres (820ft) in

The armory at Rosenborg Castle

length, a botanical gem with over two hundred plants that change seasonally.

Take a right and then a left to reach the **Rose Garden G**, which is laid out in a sixteenth-century design at the side of the palace. The statue at the end is by the famous sculptor Vilhelm Bissen and depicts Caroline Amalie (1796–1881), wife of Christian VIII, who became queen in 1839. The royal pair were happily married but did not have any children.

Now, cross the castle moat, guarded by two green copper lions. One of the original seventeenth-century beasts was smashed apart in 1744 by three soldiers to steal the silver coins that passersby had tossed in through a crack – they were flogged, branded and sentenced to a life in slavery for their crime.

History of Rosenborg

First built in 1606 by Christian IV as a summer residence, Rosenborg consisted of the core of the south side of the palace that we know today; two storeys high with a spire-crowned turret facing the city and two bays to the east. In 1611, the central gate tower and drawbridge were added. Further work between 1613 and 1615 added a two-storey wing on the north side of the gate tower; then another floor (containing the Knights' Hall) was tacked on across the whole building in 1616, along with the spire-crowned towers, and completed in 1624. More tinkering came ten years later, including the creation of an outer double staircase, which was demolished in 1758. The inner staircase, which had connected the first and second floors, was then extended to provide a link with the ground floor.

Rosenborg Castle

Rosenborg Castle 3 (Rosenborg Slot; Øster Volgade 4A; www.kongernessamling.dk/rosenborg; charge) is an absolute must-see, bursting with rich detail and unusual objects (such as a joke chair from the seventeenth century, which squirted its victims with water). However, it is worth buying a guidebook, as there is very little English information inside.

The interior charts the tastes and needs of different kings from Christian IV in the seventeenth century to Frederik IV, his great-grandson, in the eighteenth. It was the monarch's primary residence until 1710, when Frederik IV moved out. Since then, it has been used briefly as a residence on two occasions; in 1794 after the fire at Christiansborg and in 1801, when the British bombarded Copenhagen.

On the ground floor, the private **royal apartments** contain the bedroom in which Christian IV died in 1648 and the **State Apartments**, including the **Knights' Hall** on the

The King's Gardens

Royal regalia in Rosenborg Castle

The Golden Age

Spanning the first half of the nineteenth century, the Danish Golden Age was a time of great creativity in the arts. The leading proponents all lived in Copenhagen, then a small city of 10,000 inhabitants, and would have known each other and exchanged ideas. Ironically, as art and culture flourished, Denmark was suffering economically and politically. Important cultural figures at this time were the artist Christoffer Eckersberg who introduced a new naturalism and intimacy to painting; C.F. Hansen, the inspired classical architect, who was responsible for rebuilding many of Copenhagen's buildings after the 1795 fire; the great fairy-tale writer Hans Christian Andersen (see page 58); philosopher Søren Kirkegaard; ballet choreographer August Bournonville; and sculptor Bertel Thorvaldsen.

second floor, packed with solid-silver furniture and countless artefacts.

In the basement, secured behind massive doors guarded by soldiers, are the Crown Jewels. The jewels were originally bequeathed for the use of the reigning queen by Queen Sophie Magdalene, because, as she wrote in her will in 1746, 'In this royal family there have been so few jewels, and no Crown Jewels at all'.

Before you leave, visit the **Pleasure Garden** on the south side of the palace. It's based on the seventeenth-century original, in which exotic plants created dramatic impact. Exit onto Øster Voldgade and turn left. Either cross the road for the entrance to the **Botanical Gardens** or take a short detour down to Gothersgade to visit the **Workers' Museum**.

The Workers' Museum

For the **Workers' Museum** ❹ (Arbejdermuseet; Rømersgade 22; www.arbejdermuseet.dk; charge), take a right on to Gothersgade and a second left on to Rømersgade. Housed in the former Danish Workers' Movement building, the exhibition is dedicated to the history of the worker in Denmark. Permanent displays focus on daily life, using models and mannequins to tell each story: a two-room flat belonging to the Sørensen family dates from before World War I; a 1930s flat is home to the impoverished, out-of-work Petersen family; the prosperity of the 1950s is seen through the recreation of a coffee shop, shopping street and typical working family's flat; and an exhibition explores industrial work conditions. The workers' original beer hall is now **Café & Ølhalle 1892**, see ❷.

Botanical Gardens

Return to walk through the **Botanical Gardens** ❺ (Botanisk Have; Øster Farimagsgade 2B; http://botanik.snm.ku.dk; free), another lovely green

Bird of Paradise flower

space in the middle of the city.

The first botanical gardens in Copenhagen were founded in 1600. The present ones are the city's fourth and date from 1872. Altogether, they sprawl across 10 hectares (25 acres) and are home to over 13,000 different plant species. There are lakes and ponds, pretty bridges and a **Palm House**, based on the one at Kew Gardens in England. The site forms part of the National History Museum, along with two small museums based in the grounds, the **Botanical Museum** (Botanisk Museum; charge) and the **Geology Museum** (Geologisk Museum; Øster Voldgade 5–7; http://geologi.snm.ku.dk; charge).

Repair to the café before heading on to your next port of call, the **National Gallery of Denmark** (see page 62) (www.smk.dk; charge) and the pretty little Hirschsprung Collection, which stands in its grounds.

Hirschsprung Collection

Exit the gardens onto Sølvgade. Turn right for the National Gallery of Art; otherwise, head left and then right up Stockholmsgade for the **Hirschsprung Collection** ❻ (Hirschsprungske Samling; Stockholmsgade 20; www.hirschsprung.dk; charge). This charming 100-year-old art gallery stands in the grassy grounds of the Østre Anlæg park.

The paintings and sculptures, which make up an important collection of Danish art from the period known as the Golden Age (1800–50), were gifted to the nation by tobacco tycoon Heinrich Hirschsprung (1836–1908). It is an intimate museum, featuring works by the Symbolists and C.W. Eckersberg, who is credited with laying the foundations for the Golden Age.

For lunch, you could make your way to **Aamanns**, see ❸.

Food and drink

❶ Orangeriet

Kongens Have/Kronprinsessegade 13; www.restaurant-orangeriet.dk; €€€

This top-quality pavilion restaurant has views from every window of the King's Garden. Perfect for a glass of wine and immaculate *smørrebrød* on the sunny terrace, or return for a romantic evening meal.

❷ Cafe & Ølhalle 1892

Rømersgade 22; www.arbejdermuseet.dk; €

A good selection of Danish food and beer, including 'Stjerne (Star) Pilsner' that still bears the original 1947 label.

❸ Aamanns

10–12 Øster Farimagsgade; https://aamanns.dk; €–€€€

Fabulous deli offering *smørrebrød* masterpieces. The next-door bistro upholds the quality, with its innovative New Nordic dishes.

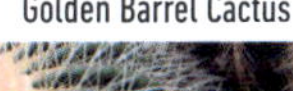

The lily-pond

Golden Barrel Cactus

WALK 6
The National Gallery of Denmark

The Statens Museum for Kunst is Denmark's national art gallery. Housed in a building that reflects two centuries of design, its world-class collection spans seven hundred years of national and international art.

DISTANCE: n/a – the whole tour is spent within the museum
TIME: A half-/full day
START: Level 1: Sculpture Street
END: Level 2: Rooms 260–272
POINTS TO NOTE: This visit can be as short or as long as you like. At a fairly brisk pace, you can cover most of it in around two hours, but you will enjoy it more if you allow a bit more time.

You cannot fail to be impressed by the **National Gallery of Denmark** (Statens Museum for Kunst; Sølvgade 48–50; www.smk.dk; charge). The original exhibition, once the private collection of the king, first went on show to the public in 1822 at Christiansborg Palace. Fortunately, it escaped the fire which engulfed the palace in 1884, and the National Gallery of Denmark, designed by Vilhelm Dahlerup, was opened in 1886. Today, its high, airy foyer, winding staircase and view through to the collections beyond are the result of an impressive redesign and the removal of a large central staircase in the 1960s.

Children are very welcome at the museum; ring ahead or ask at the reception desk about activities on offer. Prams and pushchairs must be left outside, but locks and waterproof covers are available from reception. There are free pushchairs available for use in the entrance hall. Lockers are also available for bags larger than A4 size.

Level 1

As you walk into the entrance hall, the temporary exhibition spaces are to the left and right. To get your bearings and to explore the mix of old and new architecture, walk through the entrance hall, down the steps to **Sculpture Street** ❶, which runs across the back of the old nineteenth-century building in a new glass-roofed extension. Here you'll find the latest sculptures and large-scale installations (recent works have

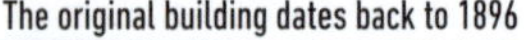

The original building dates back to 1896

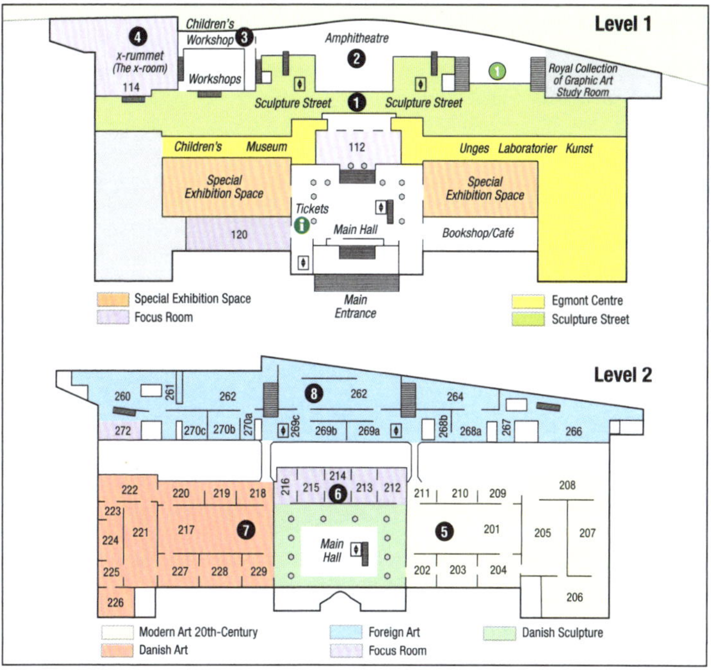

included, for example, Danish artist FOS's warped buildings, glowing yellow tents and curious machines).

Directly ahead is a set of wide steps, actually the seats of an **amphitheatre** ❷. At the back of its stage, a glass wall frames views of the water and greenery of Øster Anlæg, the park at the back of the museum. To the left is a small **children's workshop area** ❸, where professional artists help kids to explore their creativity; enter via the stairs on Sculpture Street. Nearby, the **x-rummet** ❹ contains works commissioned by contemporary artists especially for this unusual space.

Level 2

The second level is home to the collections. Take the lift in the main entrance hall to Level 2, to the landing opposite Room 201.

Sculpture in the museum gardens

European art 1300–1800

Room 201A contains an overview of the gallery's impressive collection of **European art** ❺, which includes works by Titian, El Greco and Rubens. Particularly intriguing in this room is Lucas Cranach the Elder's oil-on-wood *Melancholy* (1532), an allegorical work in which an angel apparently rues man's predilection for violence.

Three routes wend their way chronologically through the European section, tracing artists from Italy, the Netherlands and Northern Europe. The Italian route begins around the corner in **Room 201B** with examples of Renaissance and Gothic art, including the glowering marble sculpture *Head of a Bearded Man* (1312) by Giovanni Pisano and the lovely *Meeting of St Anne and St Joachim at the Golden Gate* by Filipino Lippi (1497), plus two handsome El Greco portraits and a Titian. Seventeenth-century artworks include Salvator Rosa's emotionally charged *Diogenes Throwing Away his Drinking Cup* (1651), black with storm clouds. In **Room 201E** internal torment gives way to an eighteenth-century interest in Italian travel and land- and city-scapes, with some beautiful paintings by Tiepolo and Guardi.

Route 2, looking at art from the Netherlands, threads through a suite of small rooms (211B to 209) holding works by Thomas de Keyser, Willem Kolf and Adrien de Vries, a Dutch Mannerist sculptor; and in **Room 209**, works from Rembrandt's workshop.

Route 3 covers the rest of Northern Europe. It begins with a question – What does it mean to be a 'good man'? – and answers it in **Rooms 202 and 203** with works including an altar panel by Petrus Christus dating from 1450; Cranach's famous *Portrait of Martin Luther* (the two were friends), dating from the height of the Reformation; the comic but faintly unsettling *Strife of Lent with Shrovetide* by Bruegel the Elder; and Cornelis de Vos's *Judgement Day*. **Room 204** is dedicated to Rubens (1577–1640), with portraits of *Francesco de' Medici* and *Joanna of Austria*, and his masterpiece, *The Judgement of Solomon* (1617).

Cross Room 205 and enter **Room 206**, containing examples of painstaking and detailed *trompe l'oeil*. **Rooms 207 and 208A** nod to the Danes' seventeenth- and eighteenth-century love of all things French, with work by Nattier and Fragonard among others, and lead you round again to **Room 205**, where you can check out the delicacy of the butterfly placement in Cornelisz van Haarlem's *Fall of the Titans* (1599–90).

French art 1900–1930

Retrace your steps to the landing above the foyer, where **Rooms 212**

Melancholy, by Lucas Cranach the Elder

to 216 ❻ contain a real treat: pieces by international artists who were part of the early twentieth-century Parisian art scene. Highlights include several works by Matisse (1869–1954) in **Room 214**, including the famous *Portrait of Madame Matisse* (1905), also known as *The Green Line*, which gave rise to the name of the French splinter art group, The Fauves (or 'wild animals'), whose work was characterised by a strong use of intuitive colour. The Matisses were gathered by a far-sighted engineer, Johannes Rump, who donated them in 1928. The gallery also owns 68 works, mainly etchings and lithographs, by Picasso: two still lifes in oil are on display in **Room 213**, along with a prize Modigliani, *Alice* (1918). The *embarras de richesses* doesn't stop there: other great artists include Dufy (**Room 212**); Braque and Gris (**Room 213**); Derain (**Room 215**); and Léger (**Room 216**).

National Gallery of Denmark

Danish and Nordic art 1750–1900

Back on the landing, turn right into **Rooms 217 to 229** ❼, a section dedicated to Danish and Nordic art that includes the period 1800–50, an era known as the Golden Age (see page 60) in which the arts flourished, new ideas and styles came to the fore, and, in the arts, a turning to nature and the everyday condition of the world and its inhabitants was paramount. **Room 217**, divided into six sections, gives an overview, which continues in **Rooms 218 to 220** (turn right as you leave 217F). C.W. Eckersberg, a Golden-Age giant, is well represented with *Bella and Hanna* (1820); *A View through Three of the Colosseum's North-Western Arches* (1815); and *Russian Ship of the Line 'Asow'* (1828).

Other rooms in this section are themed. **Room 221** – 'The Body in Art' – includes *Evening Talk* (1889), a study in strained body language, by the angst-ridden Edvard Munch; and Ejnar Nielsen's raw and mesmerising *And in his Eyes I saw Death* (1897), in which a hollow-eyed figure looking like a young Omar Sharif waits by a coffin, staring blankly ahead. **Rooms 223 and 224** explore the emergence

Still Life with Door, Guitar and Bottles, by Pablo Picasso

Danish and International Art after 1900 gallery

of modern-day Denmark: highlights include Anna Ancher's *A Funeral* (1891); Michael Ancher's *The Lifeboat is Taken Through the Dunes* (1883); and works by P.S. Krøyer, including the light-filled, dreamlike *Boys Bathing at Skagen. Summer Evening* (1899); all of whom were strongly influenced by French Impressionism.

Room 228 is dedicated to Vilhelm Hammershøi's trademark grey works (washed-out interiors, muted portraits and ghostly paintings of Copenhagen's buildings), and features *Portrait of Ida Ilsted* (1898), recently saved for the nation thanks to a large donation from the charitable foundation Augustinus Fonden. Imbued with light and cheer, **Room 229** – 'Willumsen and Vitalism' – contains Johannes Larsen's sun-splashed *Children Playing, Enghave Square* (1908) and J.F. Willumsen's *Mountain Climber* (1912), a statuesque woman in perfect harmony with the landscape.

Danish and international art from 1900

From the landing, cross a bridge over Sculpture Street to **Rooms 260 to 272** ❽, which are dedicated to modern art. The long walkway forms a timeline, with the large exhibition rooms overlooking Østre Anlæg park containing a chronological progression of works from 1900 to the present day. The smaller rooms on the other side focus on particular artists or themes, and pieces are rotated more regularly.

The museum's modern collection contains some particularly fine pieces, especially by the CoBrA group, a collective of postwar avant-garde artists from Copenhagen, Brussels and Amsterdam. Their colourful works tended towards the surreal, with an abstract distortion of images often borrowed from primitive and folk art. Carl-Henning Pedersen, known as the 'Scandinavian Chagall', was a founder member: his paintings are filled with cosmic imagery, dominated by abstract, otherworldly birds. Just before his death in 2007, Pedersen

J.F. Willumsen's A Mountain Climber (detail; 1912)

donated forty works to the gallery. Among his most famous are *People and Animals in a Landscape* (1942), *The Turkish Drum* (1960) and *Out into the Wide World* (1988), not on display at the time of writing.

Even better known is fellow CoBrA founder Asger Jorn, a political radical and prolific artist who produced some 2500 paintings, sculptures, prints and tapestries during his lifetime, as well as fomenting rebellion against the 'established' art world. Works include *Red Visions* (1944) and his almost fairy-tale-like *Wheel of Life* (1953), a universal and timeless theme that he took up after recovering from tuberculosis in 1951, currently on display in **Room 269B**.

Bjørn Nørgaard (b.1947), a prominent member of the current Danish art scene, is well represented in the gallery's collection. Daring and challenging works include the iconic photo series *The Female Christ* (1969) and the seventeen-minute film *Horse Sacrifice* (1970), which both caused a huge furore in their day: objects recovered from the latter can be seen in **Room 263B**. Over time, Nørgaard has become a royal favourite, designing eleven tapestries for Christiansborg Palace as well as Queen Margrethe's sarcophagus.

The gallery also holds almost three hundred pieces by another of Denmark's greats, Per Kirkeby (b.1938), who has spent more than four decades exploring broad metaphysical concepts. Landscape and nature are recurring themes, depicted with characteristically vigorous, thickly textured brushstrokes. In commenting on his thought processes as he paints, Kirkeby rather comfortingly says that if he makes a mistake, 'it doesn't matter much; I can always paint over it'.

There are several installations of the love-'em-or-hate-'em kind, such as subversive creations by Danish/ Norwegian collaborators Michael Elmgreen and Ingar Dragset in **Room 302C**: as the door swings shut behind you, *Please, Keep Quiet!* (2003) unnerves visitors with its detailed reconstruction of a hospital ward.

To take a break and digest all the artwork that you have seen, head to *Kafeteria* on Level 1, see 1. The bookshop, on the same floor, has an excellent range of art books and National Gallery publications.

Food and Drink

1 Kafeteria

Level 1; www.smk.dk; €€

Lovely fresh food, all cooked on the spot and served in stylish surroundings. The café was designed by artists Bjørn Nørgaard and Peter Lassen and has great views across Østre Anlæg park.

The gallery's airy interior

TOUR 7
Nørrebro and the reservoirs

The main things to do in Nørrebro are walking in the cemetery on a nice day and meandering around the shopping streets around Sankt Hans Torv. Weather permitting, the reservoirs are a pleasant spot for a walk or jog.

DISTANCE: 4km (3 miles)
TIME: A half-day
START: Drønnings Louise Bro
END: Tycho Brahe Planetarium
POINTS TO NOTE: It's a long walk from the centre: bus 5C from Rådhuspladsen to Dronning Louises Brø will shorten the journey.

Nørrebro (North Bridge) lies beyond the reservoirs. It started off as a staunch working-class district in the nineteenth century. It still has a reputation for political activism, and is a lively, multicultural place to hang out or shop.

Start on the city side of **Dronning Louises Bro** ❶ (Bridge), a popular gathering point for public demonstrations. On your left is **Peblinge Sø** (lake), while on your right is **Sortedams Sø**.

Walk down Nørrebrogade and turn left on Blågardsgade, passing through **Blågards Plads** ❷. This avenue once led to Blågård mansion, named for its distinctive blue roof tiles, which burnt down in 1835. On your left, note the 22 granite statues along the edges of the sunken square, carved on site by sculptor Kai Nielsen who used local people as his inspiration. Cross the square and turn right up Korsgade as far as Kapelvej. Head right at Helligkors Kirke, following the street around until you reach the entrance to the cemetery on your left.

Assistens Kirkegaard

This **churchyard** ❸ (free) is very popular with locals, especially in summer, when you will see plenty of joggers, sunbathers and parents with buggies. It was laid out in 1760 to relieve pressure on the city graveyards, which were full to overflowing after several outbreaks of plague had killed over one-third of the population (23,000 people) in just fifty years.

The main entrance is between two urn-topped red-brick gate posts. To locate the grave of Hans Christian Andersen (see page 58), take the

Paddle boats on Peblinge Sø

left-hand pathway inside the entrance and then follow the right-hand path to a map showing where famous figures, such as H.C. Andersen, Søren Kierkegaard, Niels Bohr and Dan Turréll, are buried; a little beyond, the red-brick building Kulturcentret Assistens has paper maps.

Come out of the same gate, walk left along Kappelvej, then swerve right onto Nørrebrogade. Cross the road and stroll down to **Elmegade** 4, a popular shopping street where you can browse in the likes of Foxy Lady, Fünf and Radical Zoo for streetwear clothing and accessories. For a coffee or a bite to eat, drop into the **Laundromat Café**, see 1, or press on until you reach **Sankt Hans Torv** 5, the central place to hang out in summer. There are several pleasant cafés with outdoor seating here; connoisseurs could also try coffee-bean specialists **Kaffeplantagen**, see 2.

Laundry and lattes at the Laundromat Café

Food and drink

1 Laundromat Café
Elmegade 15;
www.thelaundromatcafe.com; €
One of Copenhagen's first concept cafés, Laundromat just celebrated its tenth birthday. Do your washing, buy second-hand books, and indulge in an excellent breakfast or brunch.

2 Kaffeplantagen
Sankt Hans Torv 3;
www.kaffeplantagen.dk; €
Specialist roastery brews one of the best cups of coffee in Copenhagen. Window seats are topped with big comfy cushions – perfect for relaxing.

3 Café 22
Sortedam Dossering 21;
www.cafe22.dk; €€
Attractive decor and reasonable food. The real appeal is the outdoor lakeside seating, where you can sit and watch the swans.

Tycho Brahe Planetarium

Cross the square and walk down Sankt Hans Gade. At the first junction, you can either continue on to **Café 22**, see 3, or turn right on to **Ravnsborggade** 6, which is full of bric-a-brac and antique shops. At the end, take the left onto Nørrebrogade. Just before Dronning Louises Bro, head right down **Peblinge Dossering** 7, stopping to enjoy the view from one of many reservoir-side benches.

Continue alongside the water to the **Tycho Brahe Planetarium** 8 (Gammel Kongevej 10; http://planetariet.dk; charge), which has one or two interesting displays and an IMAX cinema.

Café life on Sankt Hans Torv

WALK 8
Frederiksberg

Leafy Frederiksberg is Copenhagen's upmarket – formerly royal – suburb, and home to Frederiksberg Slot, Søndermarken and the underground Cisternerne art space, the zoo and leafy residential boulevards. Although so close to the centre, it is a municipality independent of Copenhagen.

DISTANCE: 2km (1.25 miles)
TIME: A full day
START: Frederiksberg Runddel
END: Memorial Mound
POINTS TO NOTE: This walk works well in both directions – in summer the zoo is open late, so it makes sense to go there last; in winter you may want to head there first. You can also tack this walk, or part of it, onto the Vesterbro route (see page 30). Turn right at the top of Ny Carlsberg Vej, cross the road and up some steps into Søndermarken. Follow the path to Frederiksberg Castle and the zoo.

Until the eighteenth century, Frederiksberg was a small country village. It rose to prominence as the concept of a country retreat began to appeal to middle-class and wealthy town dwellers. These included Frederik IV who, inspired by his travels in Italy, built a summer palace in the grounds of a former royal farm at the end of Frederiksberg Allé.

This walk starts at **Frederiksberg Runddel** ❶, in front of the park gates. Every winter (November to March), there is an outdoor skating rink here. This is not far from the junction of Vesterbrogade and **Frederiksberg Allé**, formerly the rather grand private road that led to the castle. When you walk along this major boulevard you will pass several theatres, a war memorial and **Frederiksberg Chokolade**, an excellent chocolate shop, see ①. As you approach the *runddel* (square), you will pass a cemetery on your left belonging to **Frederiksberg Church**. To visit the church, turn left onto Pile Allé.

Frederiksberg Church

Frederiksberg Church ❷ (Frederiksberg Kirke; Frederiksberg Allé 65; daily 8am–5pm), with its pyramidal roof, was built in the Baroque style by architect Felix Dusart between 1732 and 1734 and is notable for its octagonal shape, the first of its kind in Denmark. Inside, there are four attractive, green-painted wooden galleries, which were added in 1864. Many important Danes

Leafy Fredericksberg

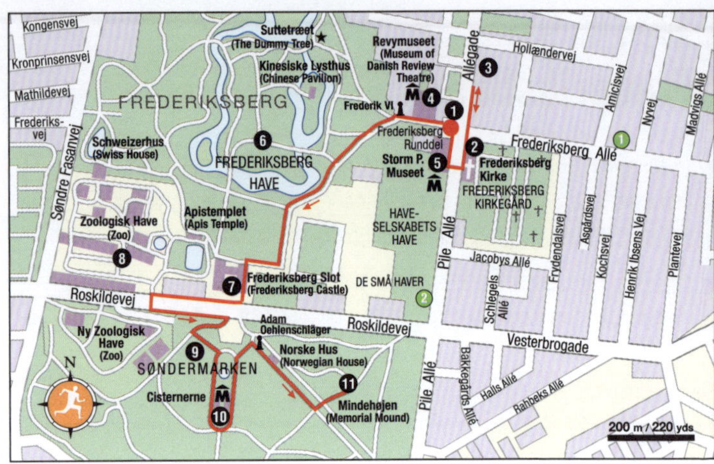

are buried in the graveyard, including figures from the Danish 'Golden Age' (see page 60), such as the poet Adam Oehlenschläger and his children.

Allégade

Before entering the park opposite, turn right and walk up **Allégade** ❸, a pretty street lined with restaurants and cafés set back from the road. This is one of Frederiksberg's oldest streets, dating from the 1650s when the first farmers settled here. Since the end of the eighteenth century, it has also been the place to have fun and in 1784, there were 34 pubs ranged along here. **Allégade 10**, on your right, dates from this period.

On your left, the **Museum of Danish Revue Theatre** ❹ (Revymuseet; Allégade 5; www.cphmuseums.com/copenhagen/revymuseet) celebrates Danish music-hall and variety acts that may be lost on non-Danes.

Storm P Museum

Return to Frederiksberg Runddel, where you will find the main entrance to the park. On the left is the delightful **Storm P Museum** ❺ (Storm P Museet; Frederiksberg Runddel; https://frederiksbergmuseerne.dk/en/storm), whose small collection is dedicated to the cartoonist and humourist Robert Storm Petersen. This witty Danish artist's work seems to combine the social realism of the late nineteenth and early twentieth centuries with the ludicrous inventions

Grey heron, Fredericksberg Gardens

of Heath Robinson and some of the cartoon qualities of Mr Magoo. You need to understand some Danish to fully appreciate the cartoons, but the museum is still worth a visit to see their visual style and humour.

Frederiksberg Gardens

If lunch or supper is looming, visit one of the three small, very traditional Danish restaurants called 'De Små Haver' (The Small Gardens), next to the Frederiksberg Gardens (Frederiksberg Have), before you continue any further: **Hansens Gamle Familiehave**, see ②, is open all year-round.

Enter the **park** ❻ through the main gate (free). In the nineteenth century, a guard was stationed here charged with keeping out anyone he considered undesirable (including seafarers and people with dogs).

Just inside the gates there is a **statue of King Frederik VI** (1808–39) by H.W. Bissen. Frederik VI, cousin to Britain's king, George VI, governed as Regent from 1784 and was responsible for abolishing serfdom in 1788. He was also Regent during the British attacks on Copenhagen in 1801 and 1807. The inscription on the plinth translates as, 'Here he felt happy in the midst of loyal people'.

There is a park map at the entrance. To the right, you will find yourself walking around the meandering canal system within the park. Turn left and walk along the side of the park for the quickest route to Frederiksberg Castle and the zoo.

The park was originally a formal Baroque garden but it was remodelled between 1798 and 1804 in the fashionable English 'Romantic' style, complete with picturesque follies. These include the **Chinese Pavilion** (free); the **Møstings House**, a listed, pretty Neoclassical house; the **Swiss House**, a little cottage built for the royal family to take tea; and the colonnaded **Apis Temple**. A colony of grey herons nests to the east of the Chinese pavilion. The males arrive in March and the females in May – they can often be seen wandering the lawns and paths. If you walk that way, look out for the Dummy Tree (Suttetræet), on whose branches generations of Danish children have hung their final, out-grown dummy (pacifier).

Frederiksberg Castle ❼ (Frederiksberg Slot; guided tours on last Saturday of each month), standing at the south end of the gardens, is now a military academy. Walk up to its terrace and admire the view along the broad axis that is part of the original Baroque design. In the nineteenth century, you could see as far as the Sound from here.

Leave via the exit on the other side of the castle and turn right, walking down Roskildevej until you reach the zoo. The park opposite is **Søndermarken**, and the far end of Vesterbro (see page 30) lies on the other side.

Frederiksberg Castle

The bridge to the Chinese Pavilion

The zoo

The **zoo** ❽ (Roskildevej 32; www.zoo.dk; charge) is not just of interest to children, especially on a sunny summer evening. It is home to plenty of animals, including elephants in an enclosure designed by Norman Foster, tigers, brown bears, polar bears and a marvellous pride of lions. However, it has faced criticism for the culling of healthy animals in what it claims is a bid to manage populations. There is a viewing tower, and a café close to the entrance.

Søndermarken

Opposite the zoo is another garden, **Søndermarken** ❾ (daily 24 hours; free). **Cisternerne** is in sight of the road (the entrance is inside one of the two glass pyramids), and the **Memorial Mound** is down a path to your left.

Cisternerne ❿ (Søndermarken; www.cisternerne.dk; charge) is worth a visit for its location alone. An underground reservoir built to supply the city with water after the cholera epidemic of 1853, its arches stretch out in all directions like a crypt and are hung with spindly limestone stalactites. It's an eerie, atmospheric space, used for changing art exhibitions and intense, immersive electronic music performances (see website).

Walk back towards the castle and turn right. You will pass a **statue of the poet Adam Oehlenschläger**, who ran around the park as a child because his father was the Palace Steward, and the **Norwegian House**, a romantic folly dating from 1787, before reaching the **Memorial Mound** ⓫ (open 4 July only) on your left. It is surrounded by tall trees and commemorates Denmark's emigrants. The words above the entrance translate, 'They who set out, never to return'. Inside, at the end of a stone passage, there is a cavern where a cupola streams light onto the life-size figure of a woman representing Mother Denmark, who is embracing her children. The easiest way to return to the centre of town is on the No. 6A bus from outside the zoo.

Food and drink

① Frederiksberg Chokolade
Frederiksberg Allé 64; http://frederiksbergchokolade.dk; €€
Exquisite handmade cakes and chocolates. Highlights include realistic-looking chocolate flowers – or how about a chocolate chess set? Also runs courses, if you want to learn the secrets of the trade.

② Hansens Gamle Familiehave
Pile Allé 16; www.hansenshave.dk; €€
This cosy old-fashioned place – with its checked tablecloths, twinkly lights and traditional Danish *smørrebrød* – dates back to 1850, when it sold boiling water to park visitors to make do-it-yourself coffee.

Lions at the zoo

WALK 9
Museums and pleasure gardens

This excellent circular walk is packed with culture and fun, taking in up to three art galleries and museums during the day and Tivoli, Copenhagen's historic pleasure gardens, in the evening.

DISTANCE: 1.5km (1 mile)
TIME: A full day
START: Ny Carlsberg Glyptotek
END: Tivoli
POINTS TO NOTE: It's easy to spend a day in the Glyptotek so keep an eye on the time if you want to visit the other museums as well.

Ny Carlsberg Glyptotek

This tour begins on the steps of the **Ny Carlsberg Glyptotek** ❶ (Dantes Plads 7; www.glyptoteket.dk; charge), a wonderful art gallery housing the collections of Carl Jacobsen (1842–1914), son of the founder of Carlsberg beer. His taste was predominantly for the ancient and classical, especially sculpture, and with his wife Ottilia, he built up one of the world's best curations of Egyptian, Greek, Roman and Etruscan art.

Jacobsen gave his collection to the nation in 1888 on the understanding that the state would create a suitable building for it. When the Glyptotek (derived from Greek and meaning 'a storage place for statues') first opened in 1897, it lay in open country with a view to the east across the swampy environs of the harbour. Jacobsen was not overly impressed, thinking it rather remote and inappropriately close to working-class Tivoli. Much of the world-class modern collection showcasing the Impressionists, Post-Impressionists and Danish nineteenth-century art was built up after Jacobsen's death.

Level 1

As you pass through the impressive porticoed facade, you can see through to the grand, airy nineteenth-century **Winter Garden**, strewn with plants and statues and home to the museum's excellent café, **Picnic**, see ①. Directly ahead are the steps to Level 2; at the far end on the left is the entrance to the modern extension.

Level 2

Level 2 filled with the **Greek and Roman collections**, the **Egyptian**

The Ny Carlsberg Glyptotek

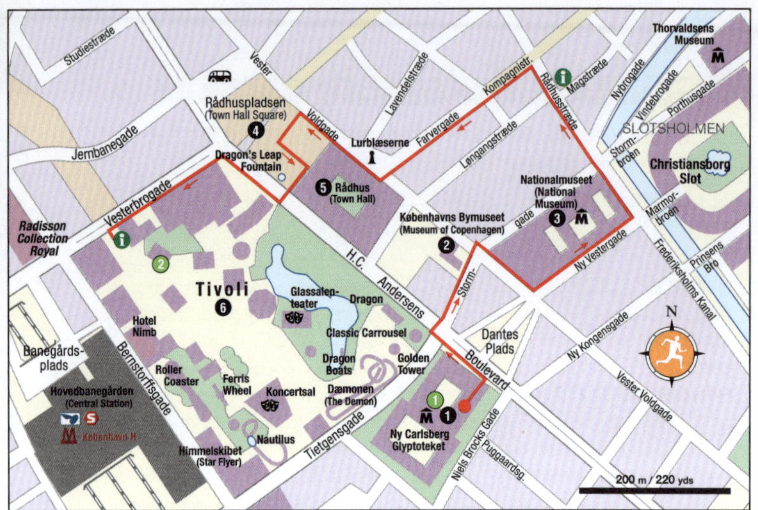

collection and **nineteenth-century French** and **Danish sculpture**. Among many other treasures, including a whole room dedicated to **Rodin**, this is the place to come for an intimate picture of the faces of the past, including such notaries as Alexander the Great, his father Philip of Macedonia, the Roman emperors Caligula (still with traces of ancient paint on the face), Augustus and Hadrian. Don't miss the atmospheric Egyptian collection, which you enter down steps as if into a tomb. Among the startling collection of artefacts are some wonderful sarcophagi plus painted models of tombs and scenes of Egyptian daily life.

The modern wing

The modern wing, designed by the architect Henning Larsen, houses a beautiful display of **Etruscan and Mediterranean art** and an impressive **French collection**, which includes works by artists such as Gauguin, Degas, Monet, Manet, Bonnard, Van Gogh, Cézanne, Renoir, Pissarro and Berthe Morisot. Look out for Degas' statue of a 14-year-old dancer (1880–1), Manet's *Absinthe Drinker* (1859), Van Gogh's *Landscape from St Rémy* (1889) and Gauguin's *Skaters in Frederiksberg Gardens* (1884), dating from the time that he and his Danish wife and family lived in Copenhagen.

The Greek and Roman collection at the Glyptotek

Dansk Design Center

The **Dansk Design Center** (H.C. Andersens Boulevard 27–9; www.ddc.dk), across the road, is no longer open to the general public, but the building, which is the work of architect Lars Henning, is worth a look. Danish interiors fans should head to the Design Museum (see page 54).

Museum of Copenhagen

Walk down Stormgade to the **Museum of Copenhagen** ❷ (Stormgade 18; https://cphmuseum.kk.dk/en; charge), which was given an exciting boost when work began on the metro system's new circle line. As the excavators moved in, all kinds of archaeological goodies came to light, some of which have changed the standard interpretations of Copenhagen's past. Expect to be taken from Copenhagen's early days as a small fishing village to modern times, via atmospheric reconstructions and interactive exhibits, as well as fascinating objects from the collection.

National Museum

The next port of call is the **National Museum** ❸ (National Museet; Ny Vestergade 10; www.natmus.dk; charge), Denmark's big-hitting cultural collection. At the end of Stormgade, take a right on Vester Voldgade and first left down Ny Vestergade. The museum is a little way down on the left.

The exhibits date from the prehistoric period through to the modern day in Denmark and includes a wonderful ethnographic display. The ground floor is home to prehistory and the Children's Museum. The first to third floors can be confusing but the rooms all run around the atrium with ethnography, coins and medals, the Middle Ages and the state rooms on the first floor; the history of Denmark (1660–2000) and more ethnographic collections (including those of the Inuit) on the second floor; and Near Eastern and Greek and Roman antiquities on the third floor. Young visitors (under-12s) will enjoy exploring the replica of the Viking ship or trying on dresses from the 'Grandma's Wardrobe' at the excellent Children's Museum.

Ground floor

The museum's amazing **prehistoric exhibition** includes unique archaeological treasures such as the **Gundestrup Cauldron**, thought to show scenes of human sacrifice and one of the world's few depictions of the Iron-age god Cernunnos; the **Trundholm Chariot of the Sun**, dating from *c.*1200 BC, when the Danes worshipped the sun, imagining it riding through the sky in a chariot pulled by a celestial horse; and the fascinating **Egtved grave** belonging

Masks at the National Museum

to a blonde young woman wearing a string skirt, bodice, dagger and hairnet. A companion grave belongs to a young man with a full head of hair and rings in his ears.

First floor

As you come up the stairs from the atrium, facing towards the street, the **Danish Middle Ages and Renaissance** is located on your left and an **ethnographic collection** on the right.

The two displays are, in many ways, similar: both vast, both charting the social and religious practices of a time and place, from minute articles to entire rooms and houses. (Both also continue directly above on the second floor.) Don't miss the **Royal Apartments** (Rooms 127 to 134), including the marvellous **Great Hall**, which date from the 1740s when the building was still a royal palace, home to the Crown Prince Frederik V.

The ethnographic collection on this floor includes artefacts from **Africa**, **India**, **Indonesia**, **New Guinea**, **New Zealand**, **Japan**, **China**, **Central Asia** and **Siberia** as well as a **music room** featuring world music and a fascinating slide presentation.

Rådhuspladsen

From the National Museum, turn left. At the bottom of Ny Vestergade you'll find the Frederiksholms Kanal and the island of Slotsholmen (see page 80). For Rådhuspladsen turn left again and take the third left onto Farvergade Kompagnistraede, home to the astronomer Tycho Brahe in 1597, until you come to **Rådhuspladsen** ❹.

The square, which dates from the end of the nineteenth century, is now a large space surrounded by hotels and restaurants. Rådhuspladsen plays an active part in city life and is the site for Christmas and New Year festivities and concerts. It is dominated by the Town Hall, or Rådhus, dating from 1905 after the original on Nytorv became too small for the city's needs. In front of it, the **Dragon's Leap Fountain** was likened to a spittoon at its unveiling in 1904: the addition of the dramatic bull in 1923 silenced the critics. Next to it the ***Lurblæserne***, two bronze lur-blowers atop a 12-metre (40ft) brick column.

Town Hall

The **Town Hall** ❺ (Rådhus; Rådhusplådsen 1; free) was built in mock-Gothic style by architect Martin Nyrop in 1905. A statue of Bishop Absalon and fantastical sea creatures adorn the facade. Inside, the entrance hall is a flurry of pseudo-Renaissance splendour with golden mosaics and a minstrels' gallery. Visitors can climb the three hundred steps up the splendid **clock**

The bright lights of Tivoli

tower (entry by tour only; charge) for an excellent view of the city, and to see **Jens Olsens Verdensur** (free), which is said to have over 14,000 parts. It is the world's most accurate mechanical clock, with an estimated error of 0.4 seconds every three hundred years. If it is sunny or you just need a place to sit down, there is a pretty **garden** (free) with benches behind the Town Hall.

Tivoli

To visit the amusement park **Tivoli** 6 (Vesterbrogade 3; www.tivoligardens.com; charge), cross H.C. Andersens Boulevard by the writer's statue to the entrance opposite.

Founded in 1843 outside the city walls, Tivoli is as popular now as it has ever been. It has a great atmosphere, and there are plenty of rides for adults and kids alike. For the brave, there are four rollercoasters: the classic wooden **Rutschebanen** celebrated its 100th birthday in 2014, while **Dæmonen** is the most extreme. The swing-and-spin **Aquila** whirls its victims at a stomach-lurching 160kmh (100mph). There are stunning views over the city from **Himmelskibet**, the tallest carousel in the world at 80 metres (260ft) high. The **dragon boats** on the lake, the **pantomime theatre**, the **Tivoli boys guard**, old-fashioned side stalls, and trees and lakes illuminated with Chinese lanterns have a romantic old-world charm for non-adrenalin junkies.

Food and drink

1 Picnic

Glyptotek; www.glyptoteket.com/cafe; €€
Lovely salads and light lunches, but especially popular for its home-made cakes. Lunch meals on weekdays and evening meal on Thursdays.

2 Grøften

Tivoli; www.groeften.dk; €€€
Grøften has been here for 141 years, so it must be doing something right. It serves traditional Danish food straight from 'grandma's kitchen' – *smørrebrod*, roast pork, fried fillet of plaice, apple pie and the like.

There is also lots of music and drama here: the **concert hall** is one of the best in Copenhagen offering ballet and opera (buy tickets in advance); the **open-air stage** hosts free rock and pop concerts every Friday night; and the pantomime theatre is free.

If you feel peckish, there is a range of over forty eateries. Perhaps the best for a full Danish experience is **Grøften**, see 2.

The Copenhagen Card (see page 132) allows for free admission. To go on any of the rides you need to buy a multiride pass or all-inclusive package. Check the website for details.

The Town Hall

Up, up and away in Tivoli

WALK 10
Slotsholmen

Slotsholmen is the oldest site in Copenhagen for it was here, in 1167, that Bishop Absalon built a castle to protect the little fishing village of Havn from the unwanted advances of German pirates. A castle has stood here ever since and, nine hundred years later, the island is still the centre of national government.

DISTANCE: 2km (1.25 miles)
TIME: A full day
START: Palace forecourt
END: Black Diamond
POINTS TO NOTE: This route is not the most leisurely, packing in lot of sights, especially if you stop for lunch. It's a great day for busy sightseeing, though.

This is the fifth castle to stand on Slotsholmen (Castle Island). The first was a fortress surrounded by a limestone wall; it lasted two hundred years before it was destroyed in 1367 by the Hanseatic League, a German alliance of trading guilds that monopolised trade in the Baltic and Northern Europe.

The second was built in 1375; in 1417 it gained in importance when the Danish king, Erik of Pomerania, made Kjøbmandehavn (now Merchants' Havn, reflecting its growing commercial success) his state capital. It was enlarged over the years but by the eighteenth century was falling down – something commented upon by visiting dignitaries – and Christian VI, mindful of his position, razed it to the ground.

The third castle, a beautiful Baroque palace, was erected between 1731 and 1745 but it fell victim to fire in 1794 and only the magnificent stables and intimate red-and-gold theatre escaped the flames (see page 83). The royal family retreated to the mansions of the aristocratic elite at Amalienborg from which they never returned (see page 49).

Between 1803 and 1828 a fourth castle, designed by the classical architect C.F. Hansen, was built. Used for ceremonial occasions and entertaining, in 1848, it too went up in smoke, with just the palace church and the riding ground left standing.

The fifth and current incarnation was built between 1907 and 1928 by Thorvald Jørgensen who, mindful of the fate of its predecessors, built its walls of reinforced concrete with granite facings. It is home to the State Rooms, the Folketinget

Aerial view of Slotsholmen

(Parliament), Prime Minister's Office and Supreme Court.

Slotsholmen in a day

Before starting the tour of Christiansborg (www.christiansborg.dk), you may be interested in exploring some of the iconic buildings that you can see as you stand at the main gate of the castle. **Holmens Kirke** ❶ (www.holmenskirke.dk; free), another of Christian IV's projects, lies across the water. It was originally a naval forge, where anchors were made, but was converted into a church for the navy in 1619. Queen Margrethe was married here in 1967.

Note, too, the fabulous edifice with the twisted spire, directly across the canal from the church. This is the erstwhile **Stock Exchange** ❷, (Børsen; closed to the public), built between 1618 and 1624 by Christian IV, who wanted to make Copenhagen a great trading centre. The building was constructed with many doors on a narrow dam surrounded by water on both sides, so that goods could be unloaded directly inside from ships. It originally housed a simple hall, which had storage space on the ground floor, and booths and offices on the upper floor. In 1625, Christian enhanced the design by adding eighteen gables and a 54-metre (177ft) spire, made up of four entwined dragons' tails, said to protect the building. The three golden crowns on top represent Denmark, Norway and Sweden. It did not become a stock exchange until the mid-nineteenth century. The traders are now long gone, and the building is used as offices and an events venue.

The Neoclassical building with the portico to the north is the **Palace Church** ❸ (Christiansborg Slotskirke, Christiansborg Slotplads; free), a lovely, light, airy affair, built by C.F. Hansen between 1813 and 1826 after its Rococo predecessor burnt down in 1794. Almost two hundred years later, in June 1992, during Whitsun Carnival, it was beset by fire again, its cupola and dome crashing to the floor. It has now been restored to international acclaim.

The ruins of Absalon's Castle

Now to start the tour proper. Peer inside the castle forecourt at the **equestrian statue** ❹ by H.W. Bissen, which represents Frederik VII (1848–63), before passing through the **King's Gate** ❺. Stop to visit the **ruins of Absalon's Castle** ❻, which will give you an idea of the size as well as the history of this site. In addition to the remains of the walls, houses, a bakery and Absalon's chapel, you will be privy to Absalon's 'secret', an ancient toilet, through which detritus washed into the harbour. Look out, too, for a wooden pipe, which was part of a system of hollowed-out tree trunks that brought fresh water to the castle from Lake Emdrup 6km (4 miles) away.

There is also a smattering of remains of the second castle, including the

The castle close-up

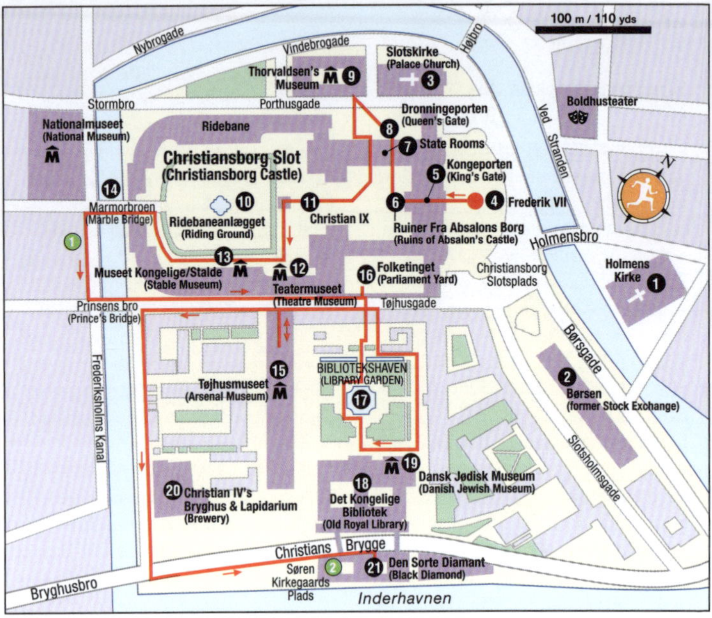

foundations of the terrible 'Blue Tower', in which prisoners, noble and plebeian alike could be holed up for years. Princess Leonora Christina, a favourite daughter of Christian IV, spent almost 22 years locked up here after her husband, Count Corfitz Ulfeldt, plotted against the new king, Frederik III. Ulfeldt was accused of treason in 1663 but died before he could be executed.

The State Rooms

The **State Rooms** ❼ (www.christiansborg.dk; charge) are reached via the **Queen's Gate** ❽, which dates back to the time of the fourth palace. They are best visited on one of the recommended tours (in English 3pm; included in ticket price), which take in the **Throne Room**, **Dining Room**, **Royal Chambers**, the **Great Hall** with tapestries by Bjørn Nørgaard, and the **Queen's Reference Library**, lined with roughly 3km (2 miles) of shelving. The guides are so enthusiastic that, if you weren't before, you are bound to be a royalist by the time you finish. Other tours offered include

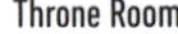
Throne Room

the ruins under Christiansborg, the Royal Stables and the Royal Kitchen.

Thorvaldsen's Museum

If you are interested in classical nineteenth-century sculpture, from here, walk through Prince Jørgens Gård, bearing left to reach the **Thorvaldsen's Museum** ❾ (Bertel Thorvaldsens Plads 2; www.thorvaldsensmuseum.dk; free) on the far edge of the island, on Gammel Strand (see page 40). This brightly painted museum, its exterior depicting a life-size scene of the great sculptor's triumphant homecoming from Italy in 1838 after an absence of forty years, houses virtually the entire collection of Bertel Thorvaldsen (1770–1844). His plans, casts, originals and replicas, plus his antiques – including examples of Egyptian, Greek, Etruscan and Roman works – and his hoard of paintings, are all here. He is buried in the courtyard at the centre of the museum, which opened in 1848.

The riding ground

Back in the Inner Courtyard, look up at the tower that dominates the palace roofline; at 106 metres (348ft), it is one metre taller than the Town Hall and thus the highest in the old part of Copenhagen.

Now, walk through to the **riding ground** ❿, which survived the fire of 1848. The equestrian statue, complementing the one in the palace forecourt, depicts **Christian IX** ⓫ and is the work of sculptor, Anne Marie Carl Nielsen (1863–1945), wife of the Danish composer Carl Nielsen.

Theatre and stable museums

The Theatre and Stable Museums are tucked under the arcade on the left-hand side of the riding ground. Both were part of the third palace and the sole survivors of the fire in 1794.

The **Theatre Museum** ⓬ (Christiansborg Ridebane 18; www.teatermuseet.dk; charge) is not

$50 million theft

Some 4.5 million books are a lot to keep track of as Frede Møller-Kristensen, an employee of the Royal Library, realised. Between 1968 and 1978, he removed 3200 items, including manuscripts by Martin Luther and first editions by Immanuel Kant, Thomas More and John Milton; nobody noticed until 1975. Møller-Kristensen sold over two million dollars' worth of books and remained undetected until his death in 2003. But his family were careless in selling the remainder and their cover was blown when books belonging to the library appeared at auction at Christie's in London. A police raid on the family house unearthed 1500 books and they received sentences of between eighteen months and three years each.

Great Hall

Costumes at the Theatre Museum

The king's doctor

Johann Struensee (1737–72) was a German doctor who was influenced by the revolutionary ideas of the Enlightenment. Convinced he had a greater calling than that of a mere physician, he sought preferment at court and, in 1767, became travelling doctor to the mentally unstable king, Christian VII. He gained the affection and trust of the young king and by September 1770, had been given the senior post of Privy Counsellor. By this time, he was also the lover of Queen Caroline Matilde (sister of George III, King of England), which sparked great scandal. Until his downfall in January 1772, he ruled Denmark in the king's name, zealously, introducing over a thousand far-sighted reforms. But he was resented and his reforms met with disfavour. In January 1772, he was arrested, accused of usurping the royal authority in contravention of the royal law. He was imprisoned in Kastellet and executed on 28 April 1772. The opulent Danish film, *A Royal Affair* (*En kongelig affære*, 2012), is a gripping account of the doctor's rise and fall.

to be missed. One of the oldest court theatres in the world, it was designed by the French architect Nicolas-Henri Jardin and has been restored to how it would have looked in its sumptuous heyday between 1767 and 1881, when it was a stage for opera and drama.

The **Stable Museum** ⓭ Christiansborg Ridebane 12; www.christiansborg.dk; charge) next door houses the collection of state coaches and carriages in palatial, marble-columned surroundings that kept the king's horses in equine splendour.

The Arsenal Museum

Turn left and walk towards the Rococo **Marble Bridge** ⓮ (Marmorbroen). Built in 1744, it is the most ornate of the nine bridges linking Slotsholmen to the surrounding city districts. Cross over and have a bite to eat at **Kanal Cafeen**, see ➊, or wait until you reach the Black Diamond.

For the **Arsenal Museum** ⓯ (Tøjhusmuseet; Tøjhusgade 3; Frederiksholmskanal; http://natmus.dk/toejhusmuseet; charge), cross the Marble Bridge, turn left and then left over **Prince's Bridge** (Prinsens Bro) into Tøjhusgade. About two-thirds of the way down on your right, the museum is housed in a splendid brick building dating from 1598, which used to be Christian IV's cannon hall. It's worth a visit for the building alone – reputedly the longest in Europe at 163 metres (535ft). The ground floor bristles with guns and artillery, while the upper floor traces the history of Denmark's wars from 1500 to the present, as well as showcasing standout items.

Arsenal Museum

The Old Royal Library and the Danish Jewish Museum

Come out of the Arsenal and turn right down to **Parliament Yard** ⓰. Sessions of the Danish Parliament (Folketinget; www.thedanishparliament.dk) are open to the public; when parliament is not in session, there are free English tours of the building. Otherwise, duck through a door on your right, where you will find an attractive **garden** ⓱, complete with pond and statuary. At the far end is the **Old Royal Library** ⓲, dating from 1906.

The **Danish Jewish Museum** ⓳ (Holmens Kanal 2; www.jewmus.dk) charts the life of the Jewish community in Copenhagen from the seventeenth century, when immigrants were rather aristocratic, to just before World War II, when marginalised groups of society began to arrive to escape the hardships of Eastern Europe. The exhibition does not cover the Holocaust or World War II; this is covered at the Museum of Danish Resistance 1940–5 (Frihedsmuseet; see page 53).

The Lapidarium of Kings and the Black Diamond

Retrace your steps along Tøjhusgade, turning left before Prince's Bridge to walk alongside Frederiksholm Kanal. Towards the further end of the cobbled lane, the ivy-covered **Christian IV's Brewery** ⓴ (Bryghus) is one of Copenhagen's oldest buildings. It was originally built as part of Copenhagen's fortifications before it was turned into a brewery to supply beer to the navy. Inside, the **Lapidarium of Kings** (www.christiansborgslot.dk/de-6-besgssteder) shelters a fascinating collection of three hundred sculptures and statues. Highlights include the equestrian statue of Frederik V from Amalienborg.

Continue your walk alongside the water to the **Black Diamond** ㉑ (Den Sorte Diamant; Christians Brygge 1; www.kb.dk/en/dia; free), the modern extension of the Royal Library. It opened in 1999 and takes its name from its shiny black exterior and slanting silhouette. The library's archives include original manuscripts by H.C. Andersen, Søren Kirkegaard and Karen Blixen. If you haven't had lunch yet, head around the corner to **1733**, see ②.

Food and drink

① Kanal Cafeen

Frederiksholms Kanal 18; www.kanalcafeen.dk; € (cash only)
Hearty local food, including *smørrebrød*, in warm and cosy wood-beamed surroundings.

② 1733

Nybrogade 14; https://1733.dk; €€
Delicious Danish lunches, including the signature herring open sandwiches alongside good steaks, schnitzel and roast beef.

Old Royal Library

Stable Museum

WALK 11
Christianshavn and Holmen

Christianshavn is one of the city's most colourful districts and the closest you will get to seeing how Copenhagen looked before the fire in 1728. It was created as a harbourside merchant town to help promote trade.

DISTANCE: 3km (2 miles)
TIME: A full day
START/END: Knippel's Bridge
POINTS TO NOTE: If you find yourself short of time, an appealing way to see some of Christianshavn is to take a harbour tour (see page 48).

Christian IV wanted to make Copenhagen the cultural, religious and business centre for the whole of the Nordic region and, as such, needed to enhance the naval and trading capabilities of the city.

Between 1618 and 1623, he had fortifications built in the swampy area between Copenhagen and the island of Amager. Five bastions were completed by 1623. By 1639 he decided that he wanted to build a town and gave the order for Christianshavn (Christian's Harbour) to be built, allowing for dockyards and warehouses alongside the merchant housing. He was so determined for this new city to be populated that he offered many of Copenhagen's wealthy merchants independence, free land, twelve years unrestrained by taxes and several other incentives to up sticks from their comfortable homes and business premises on the mainland and settle here instead.

His experiment worked and by the time he died in 1648, Copenhagen had become the naval and economic centre of the region.

Christian's Church

Start at the green-towered **Knippel's Bridge** ❶ (Knippelsbro), the site of the first bridge between the mainland and Amager Island. Built in 1937, it is named after Hans Knipp, the tollkeeper of the original erected in 1618. Note the six black, shiny buildings on your right, designed by the architect Henning Larsen, in stark contrast with the old-world atmosphere of the rest of the area. Walk up as far as Strandgade and take a right and walk down to Christian's Church.

Christian's Church ❷ (Christians Kirke; Strandgade 1; www.christianskirke.dk; free) is one of two splendid churches on Christianshavn. It was

The colourful canalside

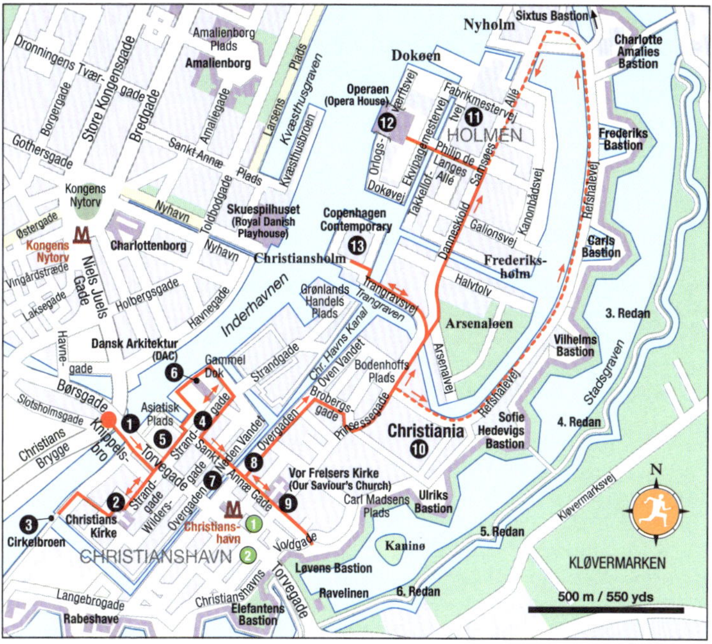

built between 1754 and 1759 by Nicolai Eigtved, Frederik V's master architect, who masterminded many of Copenhagen's eighteenth-century churches. This elegant rococo design is notable for its unusual, theatrical layout in which three tiers of seating galleries run around the walls, with the royal pew in the centre opposite the altar, technically in the position of the 'stage'. Originally called Frederiks Kirke, the name was changed in 1901 to reflect the importance of Christian IV. Today, it's also known as the Theatre Church, and is sometimes used as a concert venue, for example, during the Jazz Festival.

Cross the road and walk down Johan Semps Gade to the waterside. To your left you will see the five ship-like masts of **Cirkelbroen** ❸, a beautiful pedestrian swing bridge designed by Danish-Icelandic artist Olafur Eliasson.

Strandgade and the docks

Walk back up to Torvegade and cross over into **Strandgade** ❹. This elegant

Canal boat

Aerial view of Christianshavn

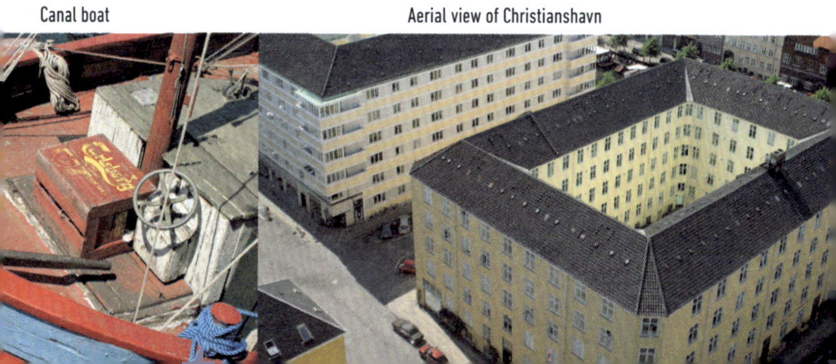

seventeenth-century street was the one of the earliest, and **Nos. 30** and **32** were the first houses to be built here. They originally had curved attic gables similar to those adorning Rosenborg Castle; these have since been replaced by an additional storey. The painter Vilhelm Hammershøi lived at No. 30 between 1899 and 1909, producing many of his trademark grey-tone interiors here.

As its name, Beach Street, suggests, Strandgade was originally right on the shoreline, with jetties and harbourside gardens. The closer to the water (and Copenhagen) you were, the smarter the address. It still has a certain cachet today, and until recently the much-revered restaurant, *Noma*, was located at its furthest end.

Head through the wooden door on the left, opposite Sankt Annæ Gade, into **Asiatisk Plads** ❺. This is named for the Asiatisk Kompagnie, which traded with India and China from here in the eighteenth century. It was also responsible for commissioning and paying for the excessively expensive statue in the Amalienborg Plads (see page 49). On the north side, the marble facade of the elongated rococo warehouse was designed by Nicolai Eigtved in 1750 and dates from Christianshavn's heyday. It is now a conference centre.

Walk past the lovely old boats and bear right, past the end of the next building into **Gammel Dok** (Old Dock). On the far side, the **Danish Architecture Centre (DAC)** ❻ (Dansk Arkitektur Center; Strandgade 27B; www.dac.dk; charge) is Denmark's foremost exhibition centre for new architecture. Housed in an attractive converted warehouse with exposed beams, it has constantly changing displays. It also has a good bookshop, and its café boats an excellent waterside view. Further up on **Grønlands Handels Plads**, opposite Nyhavn, the warehouses belonged to the Royal Greenland Trading Company (Kongelig Grønlandske Handel) and were used to store whale oil, skins and dried fish. There was then, and still is now, a Greenlandic population in Christianshavn.

Retrace your steps down Strandgade to Sankt Annæ Gade; note **No. 32** on the corner of the junction, thought to be the oldest house in Christianshavn, dating from *c.*1622. Follow Sankt Annæ Gade to the two charming cobbled streets overlooking the houseboats on the **Christianshavn Canal**: **Overgaden Neden Vandet** ❼ (Upper Street Below the Water) is on your left and **Overgaden Oven Vandet** ❽ (Upper Street Above the Water) on your right. Cross the bridge and head towards **Our Saviour's Church**, with the twisting, golden spire.

Our Saviour's Church

Our Saviour's Church ❾ (Vor Frelsers Kirke; Sankt Annæ Garde 29; www.vorfrelserskirke.dk; free) is the oldest

The view from Our Saviour's Church

church in Christianshavn, built by Christian V for the inhabitants of the new harbour district between 1682 and 1694. Dedicated to Our Saviour, it is a wonderful example of Dutch Baroque style and is particularly well known for its spiralling tower, which twists to a height of 90 metres (295ft). The view from the top of the external stairway is exhilarating but the climb is not for the unfit or acrophobic – the pine-wood structure almost seems to sway in strong winds; and, in fact, it closes to visitors for safety reasons in bad weather. Look up to see a golden ball and a 3-metre (10ft) figure of Christ (reputedly the ugliest statue in Copenhagen).

Inside the light-filled, white-walled church, tall windows are designed in the shape of a Greek cross. The cherub-covered font has a sad history: it was given by Frederik IV's childless, morganatic wife in 1702; she died in childbirth in 1704, and her baby passed away nine months later. The altarpiece, inspired by the altar in the Roman church of S.S. Domenico e Sisto, shows God (represented by the sun) and the events of Maundy Thursday, when Christ prayed that he should be spared the crucifixion.

Christian V's insignia can be seen on the entrance, the ceiling and the three-storey organ, which rests on two elephants, the emblem of Denmark's most prestigious order, founded in 1450. The Order of the Elephant was instituted in its current form in 1693 by Christian V. Royalty and heads of state may belong; the billionaire industrialist Mærsk Mc-Kinney Møller is the only living commoner to be a member. Nicolas Ceaucescu, late former Romanian dictator, is the sole head of state to have had the honour revoked. The pulpit dates from 1773 and is decorated with figures of the apostles.

Just around the corner from the church on Prinsessegade 23, is the excellent **Grød**, see ①, which specialises in sweet and savoury porridge, risotto and *daal* bowls.

Retrace your steps and walk down Overgaden Oven Vandet, passing the former **Royal Naval Museum** (the collection is housed in the Royal Danish Arsenal Museum across the canal) see page 84 on your right. The long, rococo-style building was formerly used as a school, a prison, a hospital and then a rehabilitation centre for wounded naval personnel.

Christiania

If you wish to visit **Christiania** ⑩, take Brobergsgade, the second right after the former Royal Naval Museum, and then keep walking until you end up on Prinsessegade. Opposite, spot the colourful mural-covered entrance to Copenhagen's 'Free State', a nineteenth-century, ex-army barracks that was taken over by freethinkers in 1971.

Christiania is home to just over a thousand people, out of a population in Christianshavn of nine thousand.

Christiania mural

Our Saviour's Church tower

Take a tour (www.rundvisergruppen.dk; charge) for the most insightful experience; just wandering around can be a little underwhelming. Should you decide to visit Christiania without a guide, pay attention to the signs of 'dos and don'ts' at the entrance of the Freetown. Do not take pictures or videos, especially in Pusher Street. If you observe those rules, you will encounter no trouble visiting this interesting community with its colourful home-made houses, workshops, art galleries, music venues, cheap and organic eateries, and beautiful nature.

Holmen

From here retrace your steps and divert right up Prinsessegade. The quickest option here is to wait for a No. 9A bus, which will take you up to near the **Opera House** on Holmen. Alternatively, head right onto Refshalevej and walk up along some of the **bastions**, though this will take you a good half-hour at least.

Holmen ⓫ is made up of five man-made islands (Nyholm, Dokøen, Frederiksholm, Arsenaløn and Christiansholm, now connected by bridges), which were created from 1690 for the royal navy. It is built on muddy landfill that was dredged up by convicts who walked in huge treadmills in the waterway between Copenhagen and Amager. Eventually, the authorities supplied a horse-drawn dredger. Parts of the islands rest on ships that have been sunk and filled with boulders.

Nyholm, the first island, was built to replace the naval dock at Gammelholm, which had become too small and the water too shallow for the navy's fleet of ever larger and faster ships. The **Sixtus Bastion**, at its far end, is still the place from which cannon are fired in salute, and there are several unique historical buildings still standing.

Once, Holmen was a working naval base and its workers came across the water every day from Nyboder (see page 54). They were considered so important that during the plague between 1711 and 1712, which killed a third of the population, they lived in huts on Nyholm to protect them from infection.

The navy remained on Holmen for three centuries until it finally, and regretfully, closed its base in 1993. Since then, the area has seen an increase in public spaces and housing and is now also home to four art schools and the modern **Opera House** ⓬ (Operaen; Ekvipagemestervej 10; www.operaen.dk; charge for guided tours only). Opinions regarding its strikingly contemporary design by Henning Larsen vary, especially with regard to its controversial position on the 'Golden Axis', with the Amalienborg and the Marble Church on the other side of the harbour. But whatever the

Boats moored on the canal

critics say, the building is impressive, standing fourteen storeys high (five underground), topped by a flat grey roof that blends in with the sky.

Inside, a large glass-fronted foyer frames views of the water, lit by several huge, one-tonne lamps by artist Olafur Eliasson, who crafted them from thousands of pieces of glass that change colour depending on the temperature. In the centre, the main auditorium is encased in Canadian walnut and looks like a huge wooden pumpkin. Inside, it is a masterpiece of acoustic design, with an elaborate gold-leaf ceiling made from over 100,000 pieces of 23.75-carat gold.

The building took four years to build and was a gift to the nation by the A.P. Møller Foundation, established in 1953 by a wealthy Danish shipping magnate. The behind-the-scenes tour is very interesting; the areas you access depend on rehearsal schedules, but with over 1100 rooms, you won't be stuck for something to see. If you're lucky, you'll have the chance to stand on the stage itself.

From here, hop on the 9A bus and return to Knippel's Bridge. If you have bored children in tow, hop off instead at Christiansholm, affectionately known as 'Paper Island' (Papirøen), so-called because the Danish press once stored their paper here. The whole area is undergoing a major redevelopment. An industrial building at the harbourfront has been converted into the **Copenhagen Contemporary** ⓭ (charge; http://cphco.org), an art centre with changing expositions that also runs free guided art walks. There is also a French-inspired wine bar with a waterfront view.

Once back at Knippel's Bridge, if you enjoy being afloat, you could now see Christianshavn's canals from the water by hiring a rowing boat (as Copenhageners have done since the nineteenth century) from *Christianshavns Bådudlejning & Café* (Overgaden Neden Vandet 29; www.baadudlejningen.dk); or while away a couple of hours in the local shops and cafés, notably **Lola**, see ②.

Food and drink

① Grød

Prinsessegade 23; www.groed.com; €
Specialising in hearty, delicious slop of all varieties, from fruit-topped Danish porridge to Chinese congee (rice porridge) and Indian lentil soups.

② Lola

Voldgade 54;
www.restaurantlola.dk; €€
There's a wholesome feel to this excellent waterfront restaurant, with a seasonal menu featuring the likes of confit venison shoulder and braised fennel with anchovies.

The Opera House

TOUR 12
Roskilde

Seaside Roskilde is a relaxing day out just 25 minutes away by train. It is considerably older than Copenhagen and for centuries was much more important. This walk takes you to the town's highlights, the cathedral and Viking Ship Museum, via ancient sights and then back through the park.

DISTANCE: 5km (3 miles)
TIME: A full day
START: Railway Station
END: Church of Our Lady
POINTS TO NOTE: If you are short of time, concentrate on the cathedral and the Viking Museum. Also note that restaurants serve lunch until about 3pm and then not again until about 5pm.

Roskilde is thought to have been founded in the tenth century by the splendidly named Harald Bluetooth (Harald I) of Denmark, a Viking who converted to Christianity *c.*AD 960. It is well placed at the bottom of a fjord, tucked away but with access to the North Sea. Harald established his court here and built a church on the site of the current cathedral.

By 1020, Roskilde was a bishopric, and in 1158, Bishop Absalon, who later founded Copenhagen, became bishop of Roskilde. He embarked on a flurry of construction, until there were fourteen parish churches and five convents and monasteries in addition to a brick church on the site of the present cathedral. In the Middle Ages, Roskilde was one of the largest, most important cities in Northern Europe, with between five thousand and 10,000 inhabitants and streams of visiting pilgrims each year.

Today Roskilde is a quiet market town, woken up each year by the four-day **Roskilde Festival** (www.roskilde-festival.dk), which ranks alongside Glastonbury in the music calendar. Held on a site 3km (2 miles) south of the centre, Northern Europe's biggest festival attracts 130,000 paying punters and world-famous rock and pop artists such as Bob Dylan, Rihanna, Metallica, the Rolling Stones, Björk and the Arctic Monkeys. A stone's throw from the venue is the impressive RAGNAROCK (http://museumragnarock.dk) – the museum for pop, rock and youth culture from 1950s rock 'n' roll to today's beats.

To the cathedral

From the Italian-inspired station, which dates from 1847, turn right

St James' Church

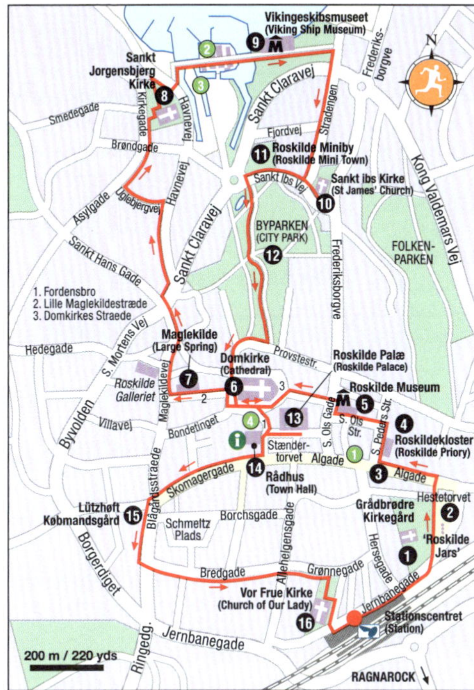

up Jerbanegade. The wall on your left wraps around **Gråbrødre Kirkegård** (free) ❶, an attractive church surrounded by a graveyard now used as a park, which stands on the site of a thirteenth-century complex belonging to the Franciscans. Take a look at the beautiful view through the gates or turn left down Store Gråbrødretorvstræde if you want to enter the park.

Walk across cobbled **Hestetorvet** ❷, named for the horse market that was held here in the twelfth century, just inside the ramparts by the eastern gate, where you cannot miss the **Roskilde Jars**. These are the work of artist Peter Brandes and stand 5 metres (16ft) high and weigh 24 tonnes. They were gifted to the city in 1998 on its 1000th anniversary by a local firm, and, as they are both storage jars and urns, represent Life and Death.

Pass between the café and the pharmacy to the shopping street, **Algade** ❸, an ancient street that has been paved for over seven hundred years. Before you follow the route down Sankt Peders Stræde, wander along Algade to look at medieval paving just beyond the *Hotel Prindsen*; the imposing red-brick seventeenth-century apothecary; and the old merchant's house opposite at No. 9. There is a good family restaurant, **Bryggergården**, see ①, at No. 15; duck through its archway to see the timbered backs of the

The royal throne

old houses. Also, peer through the gates of No. 31 to glimpse the rear of the Old Priory. Now turn down Sankt Peders Stræde until you reach **Roskilde Priory** on your right.

Roskilde Priory

Roskilde Priory ❹ (Roskildekloster; Sankt Peders Stræde 8; www.roskildekloster.dk; charge), was built in 1565 in Dutch Renaissance style as a manor house. It stands on the site of a former medieval priory, which was destroyed during the Reformation in 1536 – its bricks were sold off and reused in many of Roskilde's buildings. Shortly after it was built, the manor house was bought by the widows of two Danish war heroes and run as a home for unmarried noblewomen: they lived in great style, as a tour of the Great Hall, abbey church and reception rooms will show. However, this is still a working monastery, and individual visitor access is restricted to tours, in Danish only (see website for tour details).

Tourist office and Roskilde Museum

Out of the priory, cross the road and stroll down Sankt Ols Stræde; you can see the spires of the cathedral ahead of you. Keep walking straight on if you want to visit the tourist office **VisitRoskilde** (Stændertorvet 1; www.visitfjordlandet.dk/en/areas/roskilde), which is based inside the Rådhus (Town Hall) on the corner of the main market square (market days are Wednesday and Saturday). Otherwise, turn right at the end and head for **Roskilde Museum** ❺ (Sankt Ols Gade 18; www.roskildemuseum.dk; charge). The displays feature over six thousand artefacts relating to the history of Roskilde and nearby Lejre, from prehistoric times until the 1970s.

The Cathedral

From here, cross over Sankt Ols Gade into Domkirkes Stræde. Turn left and pass in front of the cathedral for the main entrance; visit now or on your way back from the Viking Ship Museum.

The **Cathedral** ❻ (Domkirke; www.roskildedomkirke.dk; charge) is a UNESCO World Heritage Site and one of the earliest brick-built buildings in Northern Europe. Pick up an information sheet on your way in so you have a plan.

Work on the church began in the 1170s, under Bishop Absalon, but the building was completed by his successor Peder Sunesøn, who was aware of the new Gothic style that was then emerging in France. (Indeed, this is one of the earliest Gothic buildings outside France.) The cathedral is famous for being the resting place of the 39 Danish kings and queens, going back to the Middle Ages; their chapels and tombs are a fascinating display of changes in style. There are also **pillar**

Intricate detail on the royal tombs

tombs in the sanctuary behind the choir, of royals (including Harald Bluetooth) who were originally buried in the two, possibly three, earlier churches that have stood on this site.

Inside, you are greeted by a white, airy interior with bare brick columns, medieval frescoes and some Renaissance furniture, including the pulpit, organ and altar. Before the Reformation in 1536, the nave would have been empty of pews or pulpit; instead, there were 75 side chapels where mass was said daily for the souls of the dead. To your left, on the wall to the left of the west window, don't miss the **mechanical clock** with figures of St George and the Dragon that re-enact the dragon's defeat and death cries on the hour.

The frescoes in the **Chapel of the Magi** on the south side are some of the best and date from 1462. This is also where you'll find the unique 'King's Pillar', where visiting monarchs stood to be measured – Peter the Great's height marker is the highest by far. Opposite, on the north side, are two medieval chapels that were given startling new decorations in 2010. St Andrew's Chapel gained a glittering new altarpiece by artist Peter Brandes, while in St Birgitte's Chapel, you'll find a very modern sarcophagus, designed by Bjørn Nørgaard, which will eventually hold the current king Frederik X and his wife. Encourage kids to hunt for the little green devil who, armed with pen and ink, is writing down the names of anyone who is misbehaving.

The oldest frescoes are found at the east (altar) end and were part of the pre-Reformation, Catholic side chapels. On the north side of the **ambulatory**, note the fresco depicting Bishop Absalon and a little further to the south, the tomb of the three-legged 'ghost horse', said to be jet black with blazing red eyes, the sight of which was an omen of one's impending demise.

The **choir** has an ornate Renaissance altarpiece that features scenes from the New Testament. Also here is the tomb of Denmark's first queen regnant, Margrethe I – the little bells hanging from her clothing were all the rage in the fifteenth century. There are also some beautiful stalls, carved with scenes from the Old Testament on the south side and the New Testament on the north, with odd little trolls wandering through the narrative.

To the Viking Museum

Coming out of the cathedral, turn right, looking towards the sea. If time is pressing, you can take a direct route to the Viking Ship Museum by following the signs from Skolegade. Otherwise, cross Skolegade and divert into leafy Lille Maglekildestræde. This skirts the **Maglekilde** ❼ (Large Spring), on your right, inside a wooden well house that dates from 1927 and topped by an older mermaid

Chapel of the Magi

The red-brick exterior of the cathedral

weathervane. In the nineteenth century, this spring supplied water for five mills in industrialised Roskilde; it now yields one-sixth of what it used to.

At the end of the road, turn right onto Maglekildevej, where you'll see the spring's water gushing out of the mouth of a head of Neptune. Walk past the **Roskilde Galleriet**, a commercial art gallery, until you reach Sankt Claravej, lined with seventeenth-century cottages. Turn right and first left onto Havnevej and then left again onto Uglebjergvej.

St Jorgensberg's Church

At the junction, head right onto Asylgade, which then turns into the pretty Kirkegade, with **St Jorgensbjerg Church** ❽ (Sankt Jorgensbjerg Kirke; www.sjk.dk; free) on your right. This is Denmark's oldest intact stone building, with a choir and nave dating from the eleventh century. Pop in if it is open; inside, there is a nineteenth-century votive ship model, a sixteenth-century crucifix and the remains of a 'leper's space' in the north wall, where people with leprosy received communion through a knee-high hole in the wall.

Walk through the churchyard, looking out over the lovely view of the fjord, and then down the steps until you come out on Havnevej. Turn right, then immediately left onto the harbourside, where you'll then see the wooden buildings of the **Viking Ship Museum** in front of you.

Viking Ship Museum

Arguably the highlight of a trip to Roskilde, the excellent **Viking Ship Museum** ❾ (Vikingeskibsmuseet; Roskilde Harbour; www.vikingeskibsmuseet.dk; charge) is passionately dedicated to Viking ships and sailing. The core exhibits are five well-preserved boats that were discovered in 1962 in the channel close to Skuldelev, 20km (12 miles) north of Roskilde. They had been deliberately scuttled – over a thousand years ago – to create an underwater blockade against raiders. The fragments were excavated and painstakingly jigsawed back together, to reveal a fishing boat, a coastal trader, an oceangoing trader and two fighting vessels – a *snekke* (the smallest type of Viking longship) and a great sixty-oared warship.

As well as seeing the originals in the beautifully designed Viking Ship Hall, you can step aboard re-creations of the boats at the jetty, constructed in the museum's boatyard using traditional Viking methods and materials. You can also experience a raider or trader's life for yourself by rowing out into the fjord in one of the evocative, creaking wooden ships (mid-May to September, sailing times vary; tel: 46 30 02 53 or see website for details).

For lunch, there are two options, a restaurant boat, **MS Sagafjord**, see ❷, or the museum eatery, **Snekken**, see ❸, near the entrance. If you have brought a picnic, there

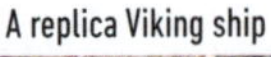
A replica Viking ship

are several benches overlooking Roskilde's peaceful harbour, filled with white sails; and if the weather is not cooperating, there are also picnic tables inside the museum.

Back to town

To take a different route back, turn left out of the museum. When you reach Strandengen, head right and follow the road to the junction with Sankt Ibs Vej. **St James' Church** ⑩ (Skt Ibs Kirke), a ruin with roots in the twelfth century, stands on your left. Turn right and follow the road round until you come to **Roskilde Mini Town** ⑪ on your right, another millennium gift to the town in 1998. The model shows Roskilde as it was in the fourteenth century.

Cross the road and enter the **City Park** ⑫ (Byparken), the site of various medieval archaeological remains, through a gate on your left. Walk up through the park for about 500 metres/yds, heading for the cathedral. It is easy to see its variety of architectural styles from this side. Don't forget to look back at the sea, with the ships' masts pointing skyward in the distance.

Walk around the cathedral into Domkirke Pladsen. If you haven't yet eaten, there is a nice little cellar restaurant, **Radhus Kaelderen**, see ④, on the corner of Fordensbro.

Walk down Fordensbro into Stændertorvet, the main square, which was laid out as it is now in 1908. On your left, the golden-walled **Roskilde Palace** ⑬ (Stændertorvet 3) is a rather modest Baroque affair dating from the 1730s, built on the site of a medieval bishop's palace. Various sections are accessible to visitors, including the excellent **Museum of Contemporary Art** (Museet for Samtidskunst; http://samtidskunst.dk; charge), with two floors of changing exhibitions. It focuses on art from the 1950s onwards, with a particular interest in sound and video installations.

On the right, the **Town Hall** ⑭, dating from 1884, is crowned by a splendid tower (*c.*1550), the only remaining part of the twelfth-

Return to Dublin

The largest of the five Viking ships found in the fjord and now showcased in the Viking Museum is *Skuldelev 2*, a 30-metre (100ft), oceangoing warship that was originally built in Dublin *c.*1040. She was reconstructed between 2000 and 2004 and, named *Havhingsten fra Glendalough* (The Sea Stallion from Glendalough), set sail back to Dublin on 1 July 2007 with a crew of seventy. The ship maintained an average speed of 2.5 knots with every second oar manned, and a top speed of 12 knots under sail. She arrived, seven weeks and 1852km (1000 nautical miles) later, on 16 August.

Viking coins

Food and drink

1 Restaurant Bryggergården
Algade 15;
www.restaurantbryggergaarden.dk; €
Good solid food served up in a cosy pub-like restaurant with helpful staff.

2 MS Sagafjord
Roskilde Harbour;
www.sagafjord.dk; €€
Lunchtime buffet or evening menu of Danish specials, eaten while cruising in Viking waters along the Roskilde Fjord.

3 Restaurant Snekken
Vindeboder 16; www.snekken.dk; €€€
Lovely, airy venue with views over the water. The New Nordic menu is heavily influenced by ingredients that the Vikings would have used.

4 Radhus Kaelderen
Fondensbro 1;
www.raadhuskaelderen.dk; €€
Good restaurant in the cellar of the town hall, serving traditional Danish food. Seating in the small courtyard in summer.

century church of St Laurentius. You can visit the **ruins** (charge) of the church, preserved under the square along with some items found during an archaeological dig.

Back to the station

To return to the station, turn right out of the square down the shopping street Skomagergade. Continue to the end and take a left down Ringstedgade. You'll pass **Lützhøft Købmandsgård** **15** (Ringstedgade 6–8; https://lützhøftskøbmandsgård.dk; free), an old merchant's house with a charming shop that is reminiscent of the 1920s, and the Museum of Tools, sheltering a collection from the period 1840 to 1950.

Keep on until you reach Bredgade. Turn left and carry on, crossing Allehelgensgade onto Grønnegarde. Head right into Fruegade. The **Church of Our Lady** stands on your right.

Dating from the late eleventh century, the **Church of Our Lady** **16** (Vor Frue Kirke; https://roskildedomkirke.dk; free) was an important, wealthy church – so much so that St Margaret of Højelse, a relative of Bishop Absalon, was buried here in 1177. It was also connected to a Cistercian convent that was built nearby in 1160. The convent was abolished in 1536, and its buildings and the eastern end of the church were demolished around forty years later. It has a pretty whitewashed interior, and the seventeenth-century pews were carved by Casper Luebbeke, Master of Roskilde.

Turn right out of the church and at the end, turn left onto Jernbanegade. The station is a little further along on your right.

Roskilde Palace

TOUR 13
Helsingør

Famous for its fictional association with William Shakespeare's *Hamlet*, Helsingør (Elsinore) is a charming town on the banks of the Sound, just 6.5km (4 miles) away from Sweden across the water.

DISTANCE: 3km (2 miles); further if visiting Technical Museum
TIME: A half-/full day
START: Railway station
END: Technical Museum
POINTS TO NOTE: You will need to do some careful planning to squeeze everything on this tour in. You may find it more convenient to do the route in the opposite order.

Helsingør is a historic town, with entire streets of well-preserved, colour-washed buildings. Conveniently, the tourist office (Havnepladsen 3; www.visitnordsjaelland.com) is just across from the railway station: it sells the Copenhagen Card, which grants access into the town's museums.

From the tourist office, turn right along Strandgade (Beach Street) to **Skibsklarerergården** ❶ (Strandgade 91; http://helsingormuseer.dk; charge), a former grocers and ship chandlers, originally dating from the sixteenth century. If you are ready for lunch, return along Strandgade to Bramstræde and head right to Stengade, the main pedestrian street, which is full of restaurants; check out **Café Kaiser**, see ①. Alternatively, treat yourself to an ice cream at **Brostræde Fløde Is**, see ②, on one of several narrow streets that connect Strandgade and Stengade. This small establishment has been serving ice creams since 1922.

Maritime Museum of Denmark

Walk down to Havnegade. Turn left and stroll round the dock in the direction of the castle, cutting along the pathway in front of the glass Culture Yard (Kulturværftet). The classic view of the castle's copper turrets is so revered that the **Maritime Museum of Denmark** ❷ (Museet for Søfart; Ny Kronborgvej 1; http://mfs.dk; charge) was built underground around the old port's dry dock in order to preserve it. Dedicate a couple of hours to the museum's absorbing collection,

Typical colour-washed houses

which does a fine job of illustrating Denmark's seafaring history; although the artefacts are somewhat outshone by the unconventional architecture.

Kronborg Castle

Follow the path across the inlets and moats to **Kronborg Castle** ❸ (Kronborg Slot; www.kronborg.dk; charge), a magnificent Renaissance-style edifice and famous as the model for Shakespeare's 'Elsinore' in *Hamlet*. It was originally built in 1420 as a fortress to protect the town and to encourage trading ships to pay King Erik V the 'sound dues' that he demanded for sailing in these waters. Today it is a UNESCO World Heritage Site, with highlights that include the ornate chapel, an immense banqueting hall, the King's Tapestries in the Little Hall, and some suitably miserable dungeons containing the slumbering Danish hero Holger Dansk.

Sankt Anna Gade

Head back onto Havnegade, take a right up Kongensgade and then first left in Sankt Anna Gade, an ancient street of much historical interest.

Carmelite Priory and City Museum

On your left, the **Carmelite Priory** ❹ (Karmeliterklosteret; Sankt Anna Gade 38; www.sctmariae.dk; charge) is a fine building dating from the mid-fifteenth century. Its church (St Maria's/Sankt Maria Kirke) is decorated with restored frescoes originally painted between 1480 and 1490, and a splendid Baroque organ from 1662.

Next door, in another priory building erected in 1516 as a sailors' hospital, the **City Museum** ❺ (Bymuseum; Sankt Anna Gade 36; http://helsingormuseer.dk; charge) has an interesting history, a Renaissance banqueting hall on the first floor and a mix of exhibits.

Spectacular Kronborg Castle

Helsingør Cathedral

The Cathedral

Continue down the street and one block on, you will see Helsingør's red-brick Gothic **cathedral** ❻ (Helsingør Domkirke; Sankt Anna Gade 12; www.helsingoerdomkirke.dk; charge).

Originally a small Romanesque church dating from *c.*1200, this was the first church in Helsingør. The current building dates from 1559 and was made a cathedral in 1961. It contains a particularly fine fifteenth-century crucifix, a Renaissance pulpit (1568) and an exuberantly carved wooden altarpiece, decorated with gold leaf.

Technical Museum

It's worth heading to the far end of town for the **Technical Museum** ❼ (Danmarks Tekniske Museum; Fabriksvej 25; http://tekniskmuseum.dk; charge), which is full of captivating vehicles, gadgets and appliances, including more than thirty aeroplanes. Some of these belonged to Jacob Ellehammer (1871–1946), who designed and flew his own aeroplane in 1906, making him one of the first European pilots.

To reach the museum from Helsingør station, catch bus No. 802 in the direction of Espergærde and ask the bus driver to stop at Fabriksvej; the stop is right outside the museum.

Food and drink

❶ Café Kaiser

Stengade 35; https://cafekaiser.dk; €€
Lovely café-restaurant in a historic building with rustic, bare red-brick walls inside and a striking yellow half-timbered exterior. The menu offers a good sweep of burgers, sandwiches and fish and chips, alongside fancier options like beef tenderloin and veal tartare.

❷ Brostræde Fløde Is

Brostræde 2; www.brostraedeis.dk; €
Denmark's oldest ice-cream parlour serves a small but delicious range of flavours. Ask for cream, jam and *flødeboller* (chocolate-coated marshmallows) for a real treat. Cash only.

Castle detail

TOUR 14
Art tour

There are three world-class art galleries outside Copenhagen that it would be a pity to miss. With time, planning and a willingness to walk, you can combine two of them in one trip.

DISTANCE: n/a
TIME: A full day
START: Ørdrupsgaard
END: Louisiana
POINTS TO NOTE: These are not the easiest places to combine as public transport isn't direct, but it is possible if you time it properly. The trip is best Tuesday to Friday, as Louisiana stays open until 10pm then. If you want to check timetables and routes, visit www.rejseplanen.dk.

Ørdrupgaard

Just 8km (5 miles) outside of Copenhagen, this is perhaps the only trip when a car would be handy. Otherwise, lace up your walking boots. The best way to **Ørdrupgaard** ❶ (Vilvordevej 110, Charlottenlund; www.ordrupgaard.dk; charge) is to take either the S-tog or the regional Kystbanen line to Klampenborg Station (20min), then hop on bus No. 388 to Vilvordevej (5min). If you'd prefer to walk the 2.5km (1.5 miles) from the station, head down the stairs from the platform and turn left. Follow the road for about 250 metres/yds, turn left onto Christiansholmsvej, then right onto Klampenborgvej. After about 1.5km (1 mile), swerve left onto Vilvordevej. Ørdrupgaard is on the left.

Ørdrupgaard is a lovely old house with a striking modern extension, full of Danish and European Impressionist paintings, with a roll call of premier-league artists, including Cézanne, Manet, Monet and Danish artist Vilhelm Hammershøi. Allow yourself plenty of time to explore the collection, as the free audioguide is thorough, and there is a pretty garden and a pleasant café. Design fans should also take a look at the house of visionary Danish furniture designer and architect Finn Juhl (1912–89), which borders Ørdrupgaard park and is part of the museum.

Louisiana

Walk (or take the No. 388 bus) to Klampenborg station. From here, board an S-tog to Humlebæk (direction Helsingør); these run regularly. The journey takes about

Louisiana Art Museum

25 minutes, and then it's a twenty-minute signposted walk.

The wonderful **Louisiana Modern Art Museum** ❷ (Gammel Strandvej 13, Humlebæk; www.louisiana.dk; charge) is a work of art in itself. Several parts are buried into the hilly slopes, so you'll descend underground only to pop out into the sunlit sculpture garden.

The impressive permanent collection features work by leading artists including Arp, Francis Bacon, Calder, Dubuffet, Henry Moore, Picasso and Warhol. Giacometti's marvellous collection of thirteen elongated figures is a highlight. The excellent **Louisiana Café**, see ①, overlooking the Sound, is another incentive for making the trip and is a good place to have supper.

Arken

On the Baltic Coast, the **Arken Modern Art Museum** ❸ (Arken Museet for Moderne Kunst; Skovej 100, Ishøj; www.arken.dk; charge) is a marvellous building in the shape of a ship's hull that provides an ideal setting for the avant-garde works of art displayed here. The permanent collection includes a room dedicated solely to Brit-Art heavyweight Damien Hirst. The museum's surroundings are being excavated so that it will eventually sit on its own island. Arken has a good café overlooking the sea. To get there, take the S-tog to Ishøj (direction Hundige or Køge; 25min), and then bus No. 128; or the signposted walk takes twenty to thirty minutes.

Food and drink

① Louisiana Café

Gammel Strandvej 13; https://louisiana.dk/en/museum/louisiana-cafe; €€

Sit by the fire in winter or outside by the water in summer at this very pleasant café. Snacks and sandwiches are served all day, with a hot-and-cold buffet at lunch and in the evening.

Henry Moore sculpture

Ordrupgaard entrance

71
NYHAVN
HOTEL
RISTORANTE IL ROSMARINO

DIRECTORY

Our edit of the best hotels, restaurants and evening entertainment to suit all tastes and budgets, plus an A–Z of all the essential information you need to know, a quick language guide, and some great book and film recommendations to give you a flavour of the city.

Accommodation

Copenhagen's hotels tend to belong to national and international chains, and offer excellent facilities and decent, if rather bland, rooms. There are many places to stay within a short walk of the city's main sights around Hovebanegård (Central Station): cheaper options tend to lie to the west in Vesterbro and more expensive ones around Rådhuspladsen to the north.

There are also several smart hotels around Kongens Nytorv and Nyhavn. A little bit out of the way, but with good views over the water, are the newer openings on Kalvebød Brygge, south of Slotsholmen. Alternatively, head slightly away from the tourist centre and stay near Rosenborg or Amalienborg: Copenhagen's transport is so good that nowhere is far from the city centre.

Early bookings via the internet are usually cheaper than official rack rates. However, it is always worth ringing up to find out if a hotel can offer you an even better price; they may be able to if business is slow. This especially applies to places that are dependent on weekday business travellers, who may be willing to sweeten a deal with great weekend rates for couples, or themed packages that might include tickets to Tivoli or the opera.

If you're staying one week or longer, renting an apartment is a practical and economic option. See the accommodation section of www.visitcopenhagen.com for details.

Price categories

Each accommodation reviewed in this Guide is accompanied by a price category, based on the cost of a standard double room in high season. Price ranges don't include breakfast, unless stated otherwise.

€€€€ = over 2500dkk (over €330)
€€€ = 2000–2500dkk (€270–€330)
€€ = 1500–2000dkk (€200–€270)
€ = under 1500dkk (under €200)

Tivoli and Radhuspladsen

Cabinn City

Mitchellsgade 14; https://en.cabinn.com/hotel/cabinn-copenhagen; S-tog: Hovedbanegård; €

There are four of these budget hotels in Copenhagen (see page 112). Space is limited (many rooms have bunkbeds) but this particular one is superbly situated, just a short walk from buzzing Tivoli. Breakfasts (70dkk) are healthy and copious.

Danhostel Copenhagen City

H.C. Andersens Boulevard 50; http://danhostelcopenhagencity.dk; €

A five-star youth hostel with a great location and far-reaching views.

Hotel Alexandra

It's modern and comfortable, and family rooms (accommodating up to six people) are extremely good value. Buy an international YHA card for the cheapest prices.

Hotel Alexandra

H.C. Andersens Boulevard 8; www.hotelalexandra.dk; bus: 6A, 33, 10; €€€€

This environmentally conscious retro hotel occupies a former apartment block dating from the 1880s. It is stylishly decorated in mid-century modern style, with Arne Jacobsen furniture, Kaare Klint chairs and Poul Henningsen lighting. It's worth paying extra to stay in one of the thirteen 'Danish Design' rooms.

Hotel Bella Grande

Vester Voldgade 23; https://hotelbellagrande.com; bus: 6A, 5C; €€€

Situated close to Rådhuspladsen and Tivoli, this boutique bolthole combines modern comfort and luxury with a classic Art Deco feel. Particularly charming are the red-and-white marbled common areas and the superb Italian restaurant, *Donna*.

Hotel Danmark

Vester Voldgade 89; www.brochner-hotels.com; €€

Located next to Rådhuspladsen, this hotel offers rooms furnished in subdued Scandinavian style. It's slightly tired, but is clean, cheap and carbon-neutral, and very peaceful for such a central location.

Imperial Hotel

Vester Farimagsgade 9; www.imperialhotel.dk; S-tog: Vesterport; €€€

A good location next to Vesterport Station and a few minutes' walk from Rådhuspladsen and Tivoli Gardens, this modern haunt is far more prepossessing on the inside than on the outside, with spacious, well-appointed rooms, as well as fine restaurants and on-site parking.

Nimb

Tivoli, Bernstorffsgade 5; www.nimb.dk; S-tog: Hovedbanegård; €€€€

This romantic seventeen-room gem is located inside Tivoli Gardens. Expect a blend of modern and antique furniture, including four-poster beds, and sleek bathrooms fitted with bathtubs and double sinks. Ask for one with a working fireplace for cosy vibes in winter.

Radisson Collection Royal

Hammerichsgade 1; www.radissonhotels.com; S-tog: Vesterport, Hovedbanegård; €€€€

Copenhagen's most iconic landmark was designed by architect and designer Arne Jacobsen. Although only one room (606) retains his original decor, the building as a whole has a charming retro-modern feel, and has recently been refurbished. Its excellent *Café Royal* restaurant offers fabulous views over the city. Rates are generally lower at weekends, when business guests leave.

Nimb's lavish exterior

A cosy fireplace at Nimb

Scandic Copenhagen

Vester Søgade 6; www.scandichotels.com; S-tog: Central Station; €€€€

A comfortable, centrally placed, skyscraper gazing over Copenhagen's reservoirs and the Tycho Brahe Planetarium: binoculars are provided to admire the view. Decent restaurant, lobby bar and gym; popular with business travellers.

Scandic Palace Hotel

Rådhuspladsen 57; www.scandichotels.com; bus: all Rådhuspladsen buses; €€€€

Another hotel in the Scandic chain, this imposing historical landmark sits right on Rådhuspladsen. Public areas retain their Victorian grandeur while the comfortable bedrooms, which are all a good size, especially for Copenhagen, are decorated in typical neutral Scandic style.

The Square

Rådhuspladsen 14; www.thesquare.dk; bus: all Rådhuspladsen buses; €€€

Stylishly decorated, this design hotel can be found smack-bang on the City Square – its executive rooms overlook the hustle and bustle. Rooms are decent-sized and comfortable, and the sixth-floor breakfast room has great city views.

Wakeup Copenhagen

Carsten Niebuhrs Gade 11; www.wakeupcopenhagen.com; S-tog: Hovedbanegård; €€

Wakeup Copenhagen is a budget option designed by Kim Utzon, with small, sharp and crispy clean rooms containing flatscreen TVs. Prices rise the higher up your room is – the Wakeup Heaven category on the top floor has the best views. Its sister hotel *Wakeup Borgergade*, close to Kongens Have, is a little nicer but less central.

Strøget and around

1 Hotel Copenhagen

Krystalgade 22; www.1hotels.com; S-tog: Nørreport; €€€€

Bespoke is the word that applies to virtually everything in this five-star beauty; from the original artworks on the walls to the orchids and designer modern decor. Highlights include a respected restaurant, buzzing bars and an attractive summer terrace.

Ascot Hotel

Studiestræde 61; www.hildebrandt-hammer.com/ascot; S-tog: Central Station; €€€

Set in a distinguished former bathhouse in the Latin Quarter, this hotel offers suites, some with kitchenettes. Rooms are a little hit-and-miss: some are fresh and stylish, while others need a makeover. Very central and no traffic noise.

Hotel Kong Arthur

Nørre Søgade 11; www.arthurhotels.dk; S-tog: Nørreport; €€€

Slightly off the beaten track beside Peblinge Sø, *Kong Arthur* has attractive rooms arranged around a pretty inner courtyard. Its friendly Danish

Scandic Copenhagen

atmosphere makes it rightly popular with returning guests. Some suites have Jacuzzis, and treatments are available from the on-site excellent spa.

Ibsens Hotel

Vendersgade 23; www.ibsenshotel.dk; S-tog: Nørreport; €€

This comfortable three-star makes a virtue of its 'Tiny' room category, aimed at guests who are happy with a (cutely designed) 10-square-metre (108-square-foot) space; while people who like to sprawl should plump for a charming top-floor 'X-Large'.

Kongens Nytorv and Nyhavn

71 Nyhavn Hotel

Nyhavn 71; www.71nyhavnhotel.com; metro: Kongens Nytorv; €€€

Spread across a pair of former Nyhavn warehouses, which were once used to store spices from the East Asia. The atmosphere is one of upmarket rusticity and many original features remain. Rooms are tiny but characterful; some have harbour views. The restaurant is recommended.

Copenhagen Strand

Havnegade 37; www.copenhagenstrand.dk; metro: Kongens Nytorv; €€€

This cosy three-star can be found on a side street, just off Nyhavn, in a converted warehouse dating from 1869. Its decor is slightly rustic yet modern and nods to its maritime position and history.

Danhostel Copenhagen City

Hotel d'Angleterre

Kongens Nytorv 34; www.dangleterre.dk; metro: Kongens Nytorv; €€€€

This grand palace is indisputably Copenhagen's finest, a luxury refuge for the rich and famous. It's also the only hotel in the city with its own Victorian palm court. Standouts include an upmarket restaurant, spa, fitness centre and heated pool.

Hotel Bethel Sømandshjem

Nyhavn 22; www.hotel-bethel.dk; metro: Kongens Nytorv; €€

In a striking red-brick turreted building, *Hotel Bethel* is a welcoming budget place. Half of its basic-but-clean rooms look out over the canal, and the building conceals Denmark's only sailors' church – ask at reception for a tour.

Hotel d'Angleterre bar

The spa at Hotel d'Angleterre

Hotel Sanders

Tordenskjoldsgade 15; https://hotelsanders.com; metro: Kongens Nytorv; €€€

A charming historic boutique dating from 1869, tucked away down a side street close to the Royal Theatre on Kongens Nytorv. Rooms are comfortable but vary in size, as do the beds.

The Huxley Copenhagen

Peder Skramsgade 24; https://thehuxley.dk; metro: Kongens Nytorv; €€€

Located in an elegant townhouse, *The Huxley* has striking modern decor and a hospitable and friendly atmosphere – nothing is too much trouble for the staff. Also does a good breakfast buffet.

The Royal District

Adina Apartment Hotel

Amerika Plads 7; www.adinahotels.com; bus: 26; €€€

Just over 2km (1.4 miles) out of the centre, but very handy for the cruise ships at Copenhagen's ferry terminal. *Adina* consistently receives positive reviews for its splendid air-conditioned apartments, with bedroom, lounge, kitchenette and balcony. Facilities include a gym, sauna and small pool.

Babette Guldsmeden

Bredgade 78; www.guldsmedenhotels.com; bus: 1A; €€€

Babette is another gorgeous addition to the family-run Guldsmeden mini-chain. It sits apart from its siblings (see page 111) in the upmarket Royal District, but the atmosphere is similarly warm and welcoming. Suite guests have complimentary access to the rooftop lounge and spa; others pay 125dkk.

Copenhagen Admiral Hotel

Toldodgade 24–8; www.admiralhotel.dk; metro: Kongens Nytorv; €€€€

Every room is different at this fabulous warehouse conversion, a stone's throw from Nyhavn. Original beams and designer teak furniture lend the hotel a rustic air. The enormous galley-like lobby has naval memorabilia and model ships on view. It's also home to a very good French-inspired restaurant, *SALT*.

Phoenix Copenhagen

Bredgade 37; www.phoenixcopenhagen.dk; bus: 1A, 26; €€€

An elegant hotel in a seventeenth-century mansion, close to the Royal Palace and Kongens Nytorv. All rooms and suites are air-conditioned and furnished in the French Louis XVI style, though some are starting to look a little frayed at the edges.

Scandic Front Hotel

Skt Annæ Plads 21; www.scandichotels.com; metro: Kongens Nytorv; €€€

A comfortable representative of the Scandic chain. Families are welcome, and some rooms have stunning views of the Opera House. Split-level suites come with top-of-the-range coffee machines. Quiet location.

A room at Babette Guldsmeden

Rosenborg and around

Hotel Christian IV

Dronningens Tværgade 45; www.hotelchristianiv.dk; metro: Kongens Nytorv; €€€

A small, pleasant hotel located beside the lovely King's Garden (Kongens Have). Rooms are neat and bright, and fitted with modern Danish furniture; ask for one overlooking the inner courtyard if you're after peace and quiet. Complimentary coffee, tea, fruit and cake available. Breakfast included.

Vesterbro and Frederiksberg

Absalon Hotel

Helgolandsgade 15; www.absalon-hotel.dk; S-tog: Central Station; €€€

The decor in this family-run place features warm, wood tones and high-end fixtures and fittings, including giant HD TVs and organic bath products.

Andersen Boutique Hotel

Helgolandsgade 12; www.andersen-hotel.dk; S-tog: Central Station; €€€

One of the most delightful choices in Vesterbro, *Andersen* has small but brightly coloured and impeccably clean rooms. Thoughtful extra touches include mini-fridges in the rooms and an evening Wine Hour so guests can mingle.

Axel Guldsmeden

Helgolandsgade 11; https://guldsmedenhotels.com; S-tog: Central Station; €€€

This lovely place is one of four Guldsmeden hotels in Copenhagen; the company prides itself on its socially responsible, eco-friendly, organic credentials. Distinctive rooms are decorated with Balinese furniture, and breakfasts are delicious. *Axel* has four stars, a more central location than *Bertrams* and *Carlton*, and a spa and sauna.

Copenhagen Admiral Hotel

Babette Guldsmeden

Bredgade 78; https://guldsmedenhotels.com; bus: 6A; €€€

66 Guldsmeden

Vesterbrogade 66; https://guldsmedenhotels.com; bus: 6A; €€

Just as cosy as *Axel*, but these two Guldsmeden siblings are further away from the city centre down Vesterbrogade: a bus or cab will be appealing if you have had a long day. *Babette* is particularly

Scandic Front Hotel

Exposed beams at the Admiral Hotel

charming, with great service and a pleasant Mediterranean orangery.

Best Western Hotel Hebron

Helgolandsgade 4; www.bestwestern.com; S-tog: Central Station; €€€

Hebron makes a decent base for exploring Copenhagen: staff are helpful, rooms agreeable, it's 300 metres/yds from the gates of Tivoli, and the excellent buffet breakfast will set you up for a day of sightseeing.

Cabinn Express

Danasvej 32–34, Frederiksberg; https://en.cabinn.com; metro: Forum; €

Cabinn Scandinavia

Vodroffsvej 55, Frederiksberg; https://en.cabinn.com; metro: Forum; €

Both of these hotels in the functional, budget Cabinn chain are located close to Peblinge Sø (Lake), a ten-minute walk from Rådhuspladsen. You can sleep a family of four for under 1000dkk. (See also *Cabinn City*, page 106.)

Coco Hotel

Vesterbrogade 41; https://coco-hotel.com; bus: 6A; €€€

This fresh, modern abode has amenities for businesspeople as well as travellers. Most of the rooms look onto an inner courtyard, so street noise is less of an issue here than in equally central hotels.

Copenhagen Island

Kalvebod Brygge 53; www.copenhagenisland.com; S-tog: Dybbelsbro; €€€

You'll find this stylish place east of Vesterbro on an artificial island. It offers all mod-cons, including a lovely restaurant, fitness centre with harbour views and sleek, chic rooms. Book well ahead to snag a double for around 1000dkk.

First Hotel Mayfair

Helgolandsgade 3; www.firsthotels.com; €€

This early twentieth-century hotel is a satisfying choice, just five minutes from the city's heart. Some rooms are small, but all are nicely decorated in boutique style; the same sense of design pervades the common areas too. Clean, cosy atmosphere and good service.

Hotel Avenue

Åboulevard 29; www.brochner-hotels.com; bus: 12, 66, metro: Forum; €€

Straddling the border of Frederiksberg and Nørrebro, this funky little design hotel has cosy rooms, a generous breakfast buffet and friendly staff. The lounge (a prime example of Danish *hygge*) is perfect for relaxing. Represents great value for money in an expensive city.

Hotel Sct Thomas

Frederiksberg Allé 7; www.hotelsctthomas.dk; bus: 6A, 26; €€€

A friendly and good-value budget option, with bright rooms and a decent breakfast buffet. Make sure you book through the hotel website to receive free wi-fi (otherwise there is a charge).

Axel Guldsmeden's luxurious spa

Hotel Tiffany

Colbjørnsensgade 28; http://hoteltiffany.dk; S-tog: Central Station; €€

A small family-run haunt offering pleasant accommodation. There's no restaurant, but each room contains a kitchenette. You can't beat the prime location, close to Central Station.

Marriott Copenhagen

Kalvebod Brygge 5; www.marriott.com/cphdk; bus: 30; €€€€

In a decent location a short walk from Tivoli, with all the mod-cons and perks that you would expect from a five-star hotel. Make sure to ask for a room overlooking the harbour.

Marriott Copenhagen

Christianshavn

CPH Living

Langebrogade 1C; www.cphliving.com; bus: 5C, 12; €€

One of Copenhagen's quirkier places to stay, *CPH Living* is a floating hotel with a splendid design aesthetic. The twelve style-savvy rooms on board this converted barge have floor-to-ceiling windows so you can enjoy the harbour views; and in fine weather, there's a fabulous sun deck too.

Copenhagen Airport

Clarion Copenhagen Airport Hotel

Ellehammersvej 20; www.nordicchoicehotels.dk; €€€

Directly linked to Terminal 3, this modern hotel is perfect if you have an early-morning flight. It has the largest rooms in the city, with floor-to-ceiling windows looking over the coast, a swimming pool and a spa and wellness centre.

Crowne Plaza Copenhagen Towers

Ørestads Boulevard 114–118; www.ihg.com/crowneplaza; €€€

Super-sleek rooms and amazing views over Amager (especially at night). Careful environmental consideration went into the building of this hotel – it contains Denmark's first groundwater-based heating system and the largest solar panels in Scandinavia. A free shuttle bus runs to the airport.

Copenhagen Island

Clarion Copenhagen Airport Hotel

Restaurants

Copenhagen has around two thousand restaurants scattered all over the city, often in the most unlikely of places. The old butchers' district, Kødbyen, has a dense cluster of eating and drinking spots and comes to life at night. The quiet residential streets of Christianshavn and Holmen shelter a particularly high number of top-class restaurants. Otherwise, you can pick and choose according to what district you're in and what your purse can bear.

Fifteen restaurants in Copenhagen share a total of 26 Michelin stars between them (as of 2024), marking it as easily the leading Nordic city in terms of recognition; Stockholm is a distant second, with sixteen stars. As of 2024, sixteen Copenhagen establishments were also awarded a Bib Gourmand for top-class dining at a more affordable price. Many have fixed-price menus: the greater the number of courses, proportionately the cheaper your meal becomes. If you are on a budget, eat in a café where a couple of unpretentious dishes will set you back around 250dkk, or make a beeline for the *pølsevogn* sausage vans found all over town.

In a city stuffed with restaurants, there aren't many places that cater solely to vegetarians, though there are several raw-food cafés where you can eat super-healthy plant-based lunches. Plus, some of the city's top kitchens will rustle up a meat-free alternative if given advance notice.

Note that Copenhagen's restaurants generally take a well-earned rest on Sundays (and some also on Mondays).

Price categories

Each restaurant and café reviewed in this Guide is accompanied by a price category, based on the cost of a three-course meal (or similar) for one, excluding wine.

€€€€ = over 600dkk (over €80)
€€€ = 450–600dkk (€60–€80)
€€ = 300–450dkk (€60–€60)
€ = under 300dk (under €60)

Tivoli and Rådhuspladsen

A Hereford Beefstouw

Tivoli, Vesterbrogade 3; https://beefstouw.com; €€€

A chain with a difference: long-standing favourite *A Hereford Beefstouw* invests a percentage of its profits into quality artworks that adorn its restaurants. Juicy steaks and seafood dishes are cooked to order, while an on-site brewery provides glasses of frothy beer.

Grøften

Tivoli; www.groeften.dk; €€

A Tivoli stalwart since 1874, serving traditional food to generations of Danes. Come here for open sandwiches

Caviar at Restaurant Koefoed

at lunchtime, or to sample its speciality dish, a beetroot borsch. It's big but cosy and is run with smiling efficiency and real kindness to kids.

Nimb

Berstorffsgade 5; www.nimb.dk; €€€

The wonderful Moorish Palace in Tivoli shelters a hotel and three restaurants under its roof: a family-friendly brasserie, a bar and grill serving steaks and cocktails, and a French-inspired bistro.

Vesterbro and Frederiksberg

Formel B

Vesterbrogade 182, Vesterbro; https://formelfamily.dk/formelb/en; €€€€

A charming Michelin-starred restaurant with a fortnightly changing menu offering dishes such as Danish cod with watercress, dandelion and cod roe, or monkfish with snails, mushrooms and basil. Summer terrace for outdoor dining.

Hija de Sanchez

Slagterboderne 8; https://lovesanchez.com; €€

Helmed by a former *Noma* chef, *Hija de Sanchez* serves the best tacos in town from a tiny plot in the Meatpacking District. The menu also includes fancier Mexican-infused options such as caviar with coriander and serrano chilli, and clamato oysters.

Kødbyens Fiskebar

Flæsketorvet 100, Vesterbro; http://fiskebaren.dk; €€

This fashionable bistro, with its chic urban interior and mesmerising jellyfish tank, serves superb fresh fish and shellfish: poached cockles, Limfjorden oysters and blue mussels, cod from the Kattegat and razor clams.

Beef Wellington at Nimb

Maple

Vesterbrogade 24; www.themaple.dk; €€

This casual dining spot serves basic, comforting dishes done well – mushroom risotto, seared seabass, pork ribs and the like – accompanied by a good beer selection.

Fine dining at Formel B

Catch of the day at Kødbyens Fiskebar

Mielcke & Hurtigkarl

Frederiksberg Runddel 1; www.mhcph.com; €€€€

This experimental gourmet place is located in the beautiful rose gardens of Frederiksberg Park. The intimate interior is great for romantic dinners, but the terrace is the place to be on a fine day. The restaurant has its own herb garden, which informs the ever-changing tasting menu.

Mother

Høkerboderne 9-15; www.mother.dk; €

Mother is one of the best-value restaurants in the cool Kødbyen area. It serves scrumptious sourdough pizzas, made in Neapolitan style, to hungry crowds. Reservations are only taken up to 8pm, then it's a free-for-all.

Neighbourhood

Istedgade 27; www.neighbourhood.dk; €

This fabulous Vesterbro pizzeria serves organic pizzas made with half the normal amount of dough but at least double the flavour. Innovative toppings include pumpkin sausage, garlic-roasted Argentinian giant shrimp, and chilli salami. Communal seating and a young cheery vibe. Another branch is on Frederiksborggade 20D.

Paté Paté

Slagterboderne 1; www.patepate.dk; €€

Cosy, candlelit *Paté Paté* is a sociable place to dine. Spanish and Moroccan dishes, including plates of tapas, are served at big shared tables. You can stop by for a breakfast croissant, but it really comes into its own at night.

Restaurant Klubben

Enghavevej 4; www.restaurant-klubben.dk; €

This pub is a little too rough and ready to tempt tourists not already in the know. Sit at a wobbly table with plastic tablecloth and feast on huge portions of traditional home cooking, such as *frikadeller* with creamed cabbage and beetroot or the traditional Danish herring plate.

The Latin Quarter, Strøget and around

Basara Sushi

Østergade 52; https://basara.dk; €€€

An excellent and stylish Japanese haunt specialising in sushi made from

Mielcke & Hurtigkarl's romantic dining room

ingredients that have been farmed or fished using sustainable principles. The wagyu and miso soups are also fantastic, as is the tempura.

Det Lille Apotek

Store Kannikestræde 15; www.detlilleapotek.dk; €€

The 'Little Pharmacy' is Copenhagen's oldest cellar restaurant, with crooked walls and one-off antiques. It claims many writers as former patrons, including Hans Christian Andersen and Ludvig Holberg, and plates up hearty Danish fish and meat dishes. A favourite with students.

Høst

Nørre Farimagsgade 41; https://cofoco.dk/en/hoest; €€€

An affordable alternative to the city's storied Michelin-starred restaurants, *Høst* serves delicious tasting menus that are a fine example of the voguish New Nordic cuisine. Offerings change with the seasons, but may include lobster tail with morels, or pear with birchbark. There is a vegetarian option too.

Kobenhavner Cafeen

Badstuestræde 10; https://københavnercafeen.dk/en; €

This small joint has an old-time atmosphere and a traditional menu to go with it; *flæskesteg* (roasted pork, a Christmas speciality); *frikadeller* (meatballs); grilled plaice; and a daily two-person plate of marinated salmon, herring, shrimp, meatballs, vegetables and baked bread for 255dkk.

La Galette

Larsbjørnsstræde 9; www.lagalette.dk; €

Family-friendly *La Galette* sells delicious savoury and sweet crêpes, prepared by a genuine Frenchman. Wash them down with a cup of crisp, dry Breton cider.

Marv & Ben

Snaregade 4; www.marvogben.dk; €€

This Nordic gastropub takes a great deal of pride in producing succulent, flavour-packed dishes based on seasonal ingredients: duck breast with chestnuts and sorrel, haddock served with cockles and a smidgen of seaweed, or juicy slow-roasted pork.

Restaurant Gabrielle

Vestergade 3; https://norrlyst.dk/gabrielle-2; €€

If you grow weary of *smørrebrød* and *stegt flæsk*, a plateful of French bistro comfort food might be just what you're after. Tasty, traditional dishes include beef tenderloin with marrow cream, and beef tartare with capers and tarragon mayo.

Riz Raz

Kompanistræde 20; www.rizraz.dk; €

This attractive Mediterranean restaurant is very popular and offers an excellent and varied vegetarian buffet. The cuisines of Lebanon, Morocco and Italy are all inspirations. There are some meat dishes too.

Høst

The kitchen at Marv & Ben

Tight CPH

Hyskenstræde 10; www.tight-cph.dk; €€

One of Copenhagen's most beloved restaurants, *Tight* offers attractive raw-brick and warm wood surrounds, a lively atmosphere and great grub. Try the mussels and crab cakes for starters, followed by surf 'n' turf or a rack of juicy barbecue ribs, glazed in maple syrup.

Kongens Nytorv, Nyhavn and around

Nyhavns Færgekro

Nyhavn 5; www.nyhavnsfaergekro.dk; €€

Based in the old White Star Line office (of *Titanic* fame), unpretentious *Færgekro* is set in an eighteenth-century building and serves good traditional food. It's especially popular at lunchtime for its *smørrebrød* and excellent herring buffet.

Punk Royale

Dronningens Tværgade 10; www.punkroyale.se; €€€€

This stylish, playful place offers a unique take on the set-menu dining experience, with a high degree of audience participation – there's music and cabaret, and you're invited to eat from each other's hands. The food is artfully presented and features high-end dishes like caviar and green curry oysters.

Restaurant Koefoed

Landgreven 3; www.restaurant-koefoed.dk; €€€€

The classy slow-food menu specialises in food from the Danish island of Bornholm. Diners are treated to fish prepared in Allinge's famous smokehouses, beer from the Svaneke brewery and Bornholm cheeses. Enquiring minds ask, "Where is its Michelin star?".

Rosenborg and around

Ankara

Krystalgade 8; http://ankaracity.dk; €

Extensive Turkish buffet adapted for Danish tastes. In a city of expensive restaurants, the evening spread here is a bargain at 139dkk.

AOC

Dronningens Tværgade 2; www.restaurantaoc.dk; €€€€

In a beautiful vaulted seventeenth-century cellar dining room, diners are served five, seven or ten courses from New Nordic tasting menus that change with the seasons. A typical dish might be venison with black trumpet mushrooms and fermented parsnip.

Bistro Boheme

Esplanaden 8; https://bistroboheme.dk; €€€€

This upscale French bistro offers a high-end alternative to the ubiquitous New Nordic options. In a cosy environment decorated with antiques from Parisian flea markets, patrons feast on classic dishes like lobster bisque and beef tartare; the Scandi fondness for game meats is incorporated with dishes like baked pigeon.

Alchemist

Kong Hans Kælder

Vingårdstræde 6; www.konghans.dk; €€€€

Set in Copenhagen's oldest building, mentioned in medieval texts. In the nineteenth century, Hans Christian Andersen lived in its garret. The French-influenced menu has an emphasis on simplicity and fresh ingredients; expect dishes like roasted langoustines with black salsify; glazed turbot with rosehip; and foie gras with Danish apple balsamic vinegar.

Pluto

Borgergade 16; www.restaurantpluto.dk; €€

A great place for a relaxed night out with lots of little dishes to swap and share. The food is Nordic tapas, best experienced in the good-value twelve-course tasting menu (550dkk).

Restaurant Godt

Gothersgade 38; www.restaurant-godt.dk; €€€€

Godt means 'good', something of an understatement for this family-run, twenty-seat gastronomic restaurant. The cuisine is European, with daily four- and five-course seasonal menus; the wine list is mainly French. Reservations are advised.

Restaurant Schønemann

Hauser Pl. 16; www.restaurantschonnemann.dk; €€€€

One of the city's oldest restaurants has been heralded for its traditional yet relaxed dining experience, which combines classic *smørrebrød* (open sandwiches) with quality Danish beer in a refined pub-like environment. The pickled herring option is particularly good.

Exquisite presentation at Kiin Kiin

San Giorgio

Rosenborggade 7 (near the Kultorvet); www.san-giorgio.dk; €€€

Beautifully decorated with whitewashed walls, dark wood furniture, chandeliers, candles and crisp white tablecloths, *San Giorgio* offers authentic Sardinian cuisine that is very much more than just pizza and pasta. Three fixed menus (starting from 430dkk) give you a choice on price.

Stylish cellar restaurant AOC

Amalienborg and around

Café Oscar

Bredgade 58; https://cafeoscar.dk; €€€

This elegant yet laid-back haunt is a favourite for its classic bistro-style cuisine, which combines French and Danish influences in its high-quality but unfussy dishes. Highlights include open sandwiches (curried herring is always a good choice), ribeye steak, and a seafood 'hotdog' with crayfish and avocado cream.

Madklubben Bistro de Luxe

Store Kongensgade 66; http://madklubben.dk/bistro-de-luxe; €

If you want to dine out in Copenhagen in civilised style but don't have a bottomless wallet, try this relaxed and unpretentious spot. It keeps costs low by offering a basic (but high-quality) menu, with surcharges for more luxurious items such as lobster and smoked duck.

Rebel

Store Kongensgade 52; www.restaurantrebel.dk; €€€

Halfway between Amalienborg and Rosenborg, *Rebel* offers delicious food, an excellent wine list and informal but attentive service. Choose from the list of savoury and sweet 'servings', which cost around 145dkk; four are recommended for a satisfying dining experience. Alternatively, there's a seven-course tasting menu including wine (must be pre-ordered), which will set you back 745dkk per person.

Slotsholmen and south of Strøget

Rio Bravo

Vester Voldgade 86; www.riobravo.dk; €€

This popular place is a favourite among late-night revellers. It's a no-nonsense, cowboy-style steakhouse, where even the seats at the bar are saddles. The kitchen stays open until 4am daily.

Sorgenfri

Brolæggerstræde 8; https://cafesorgenfri.dk; €

This 150-year-old *frokost* restaurant, tucked in a basement just north of Christiansborg Castle, is a good old-fashioned choice. It provides a very Danish experience of *smørrebrød*, beer and snaps, plus other traditional dishes like fried plaice, roast pork and meatballs served with red cabbage.

Tårnet

Christiansborg Slot; http://taarnet.dk; €€€

Set in the tower of the Danish Parliament, this is one of the more unusually located of Copenhagen's restaurants. Try to snag a table by the window for great city views. The modern Danish menu uses local produce and changes with the seasons.

Christianshavn and Holmen

Alchemist

Refshalevej 173C; https://alchemist.dk; €€€€

This remarkable two-Michelin-starred restaurant offers Copenhagen's most immersive dining experience. Multimedia audiovisual installations

Modern Danish cuisine at Tårnet

accompany the food, which elevates exquisite and unusual ingredients – langoustine, caviar, farmed butterflies – into works of culinary art.

Kadeau

Wildersgade 10B; www.kadeau.dk; €€€€

With two Michelin stars and an additional green star for sustainability, *Kadeau* takes the Nordic focus on seasonality to new heights. Winter menus are heavy on seafood, pickles and garden-grown herbs, while summer counterparts make full use of the foraged bounty of the island of Bornholm. Dishes change constantly but might include stone-grilled oyster with pine nuts, or wild mushroom soup with pickled cucumbers.

No. 2

Nicolai Eigtvedsgade 32; www.nummer2.dk; €€€

From the same stable as gourmet restaurant *AOC*, this relaxed Nordic bistro offers a seasonal menu centred around Danish produce. You choose four dishes from the offering, which may include mallard with kale or sea buckthorn with rosehip and salt caramel. Harbour bus no. 991 or 992 drops you right outside the door.

Viva

Langebrogade kaj 570; www.restaurantviva.dk; €

Moored by the Langebro bridge, this floating restaurant serves Mediterranean-inspired food with beautiful harbour views. It's a great spot for a romantic dinner – ask for a table on the top deck for the best vistas.

Nørrebro and Østerbro

Geranium

Per Henrik Lings Allé 4; http://geranium.dk; €€€€

The proud bearer of three Michelin stars, *Geranium* is a little out of the way, on the eighth floor of a sports stadium overlooking Fælledparken, but it's well worth the journey. Chef Rasmus Kofoed is a Bocuse d'Or championship winner: one of his signature dishes is salted hake, parsley stems and Finnish caviar in buttermilk.

Kiin Kiin

Guldbergsgade 21; www.kiin.dk; €€€€

The name means 'come and eat' – a hard offer to turn down. This is the first Asian restaurant in Denmark to win a Michelin star, offering a modern Thai five-course menu in a lovely ambience. Romantics should book Table 9, the most private corner.

Oysters & Grill

Sjællandsgade 1B; http://cofoco.dk/en/restaurants/oysters-and-grill; €

A relaxed, rustic bar-restaurant that does what it says on the tin. Pick between mussels, razor clams, soft-shell crab, shrimp or, of course, oysters, or plump for grilled steak or sea bream. It has a rough-and-ready concrete-and-vinyl decor but a friendly atmosphere.

Sleek Danish design at Geranium

Nightlife

Here are our picks for some of the hottest bars and clubs in the city. There are always new places popping up – chat to friendly locals to find out about the latest spots. Many of Copenhagen's best hangouts blur the line between bar and restaurant: often when the nibbles have been cleared away and the kitchen closes, a place will slide smoothly into club mode, staying open late into the night.

Bars and pubs

Bibendum

Nansensgade 45; www.bibendum.dk

Oenophiles should beeline for this pleasing bar, run by a wine importer. There are 134 varieties to choose from, sourced from all over the globe; and 33 of them are available by the glass. The staff are very knowledgeable, and the small food menu pairs well with wining: tapas is a speciality.

The Brass Monkey

Enghavevej 31; www.brassmonkey.dk

The tiki bar *Brass Monkey* comes as close as Scandinavia ever does to dubious taste. Bartenders don eye-watering Hawaiian shirts, and cocktails (based on rum, rum and more rum) are served in goblets shaped like ceramic skulls, zombies and Rapa Nui moai-style heads.

Eiffel Bar

Wildersgade 58; tel: 32 57 70 92

This old drinking den, which has been running in its present form for fifty years, makes no concessions to the twenty-firstt century. It's decorated with anachronistic symbols of Paris, and sells cheap beer to retired sailors and local students.

Hviids Vinstue

Kongens Nytorv 19; http://hviidsvinstue.dk

Cosy, atmospheric and pub-like, Copenhagen's oldest wine bar dates from 1723. In winter, sit in the wood-panelled interior; in summer, ask for a table outside.

K Bar

Ved Stranden 20; www.k-bar.dk

Close to Højbro Plads, this teeny, tiny bar promotes 'København, kærlighed and kocktails' (Copenhagen, love and cocktails). It's renowned for martinis – there are thirteen different varieties on the menu.

Taphouse

Lavendelstræde 15; http://taphouse.dk

The *Taphouse*, near Rådpladsen, has the largest selection of on-tap beers (61) in Europe. It's not just about quantity either – selected ales come from micro- and craft breweries the length and breadth of Denmark and beyond.

Microbreweries

BrewPub

Vestergade 29; www.brewpub.dk

One of many stylish bars in the city

This pub, in snug seventeenth-century premises near to the Rådhus, brews its own pilsner-style beers in the basement. There are usually seven on tap, plus another seven from other Danish microbreweries, as well as a huge choice of bottled beers. True aficionados can take a tour of the brewery itself (6pm Mondays; charge; bookings essential).

Nørrebro Bryghus

Ryesgade 3; www.noerrebrobryghus.dk

This super microbrewery has won awards for its beers, which you can sample at the bar or (in fine weather) at tables on the street; but it's not all about getting tipsy in the sunshine. The *Bryghus* also offers a creative food menu specially designed to pair with the hoppy, malty flavour of its amber brews.

Distinctive rum bottles at Brass Monkey

Nightclubs

Jolene

Flæsketorvet 81–5; www.facebook.com/@JoleneBar

This lo-fi beery place in the Kødbyen district is run by two Icelandic women, who bring Iceland's characteristic eccentricity to one of Copenhagen's coolest clubs. It's loud and curious, with flea-market decor and party-hard youngsters. Music on weekdays is described as 'alternative dark-sided seven inches and tunes to watch girls cry', while at weekends DJs play hip-hop, indie, pop and electronica.

Vega Nightclub

Enghavevej 40; www.vega.dk; charge

This huge complex of bars, clubs and music venues has everything that you require for a night out. The mainstream nightclub has wild lightshows and DJs. An impressive list of top international acts, including Prince, Kylie and Bowie, have performed here.

Jazz clubs

Mojo's

Løngangstræde 21C; www.mojo.dk; charge

This intimate place is an exciting jazz venue, known for its laid-back blues and quality performers. It has live music every night of the week, but fills up fast: the best way to assure entry is to book a table ahead of time.

Fans enjoy some live music

Danes know how to party

Essentials

Accessible travel

The Danes are generally very thoughtful about customers' needs but not all hotels are suitable for disabled travellers. Contact the Copenhagen tourist office (www.visitcopenhagen.com) for information on hotels, transport, museums and attractions. See also www.visitdenmark.com (look for 'special travel' in the 'Denmark A–Z' section).

For wheelchair users travelling by regional train (including the airport) contact the **DSB Handicap Service** (tel: 70 13 14 18; www.dsb.dk). All train and metro stations have lifts and ramps, and most buses have collapsible ramps for the middle doors and a call button. Many cinemas and theatres have hearing loops; call venues for details. Most taxi firms offer specialised transport, but book ahead; try **Taxa4x35** (tel: 45 35 35 35 35; www.taxa.dk).

Budgeting for your trip

Money-saving tips. All national museums are free for under-18s, some have one day a week where admission is free. A Copenhagen Card (see page 132) can be good value. A free three-hour city tour leaves at 11am from the Rådhus steps – look out for the bright-green umbrella (for more free walking tours see www.copenhagenfreewalkingtours.dk). Alternatively, climb the Christiansborg Palace tower for magnificent views of the city. To save money on a bus tour, hop on bus 11A which stops at the museums and major attractions. Gardens and parks, including the Botanical Gardens, are also free to visit, as are harbour baths in summer. Many restaurants offer a good-value *dagens ret* (daily special).

Accommodation. Youth-hostel dormitory bed: 300–600dkk. For a double room with breakfast in high season, expect to pay 1500–2500dkk for a mid-range hotel and over 3000dkk for a high-end hotel.

Eating out. Three-course evening meal (set menu) in a mid-range restaurant: around 380dkk. Drinks: coffee 45dkk, beer 45–60dkk and soft drinks 35dkk.

Entertainment. Cinema 100dkk; Royal Danish Opera tickets 125–995dkk; nightclub entry 70–450dkk; Tivoli Gardens: free admission for children under 8, others 120dkk, multi-ride pass 250dkk.

Flights. Air tickets to Copenhagen vary greatly depending on carrier, flight availability and season. Budget carrier easyJet (www.easyjet.com) has peak-season return flights from London Gatwick for £100–250 (in low season prices drop to £50 or even less). Norwegian Air

Shoppers on Kobmagergade

(www.norwegian.com) has similar flights for around £250 (high season).

Business hours

Shops are generally open Monday–Thursday 10am–6pm, Friday until 7pm; Saturday 10am–4pm; Sunday noon–4pm. Department stores and large supermarkets, as well as newspaper and tobacco kiosks, typically have longer opening hours; commercial centres and department stores also stay open on Sunday. **Museums** often open late one night a week (usually Wednesday) and are closed on Monday. **Banks** are usually open Monday–Friday 9.30/10am–4pm; some until 5.30/6pm Thursday. They are closed Saturday and Sunday and on public holidays. If you are looking to exchange money out of usual hours, **Den Danske Bank** at Copenhagen Airport is open 5am–10pm and **Forex** at Hovedbånegard is open 8am–9pm. **Office hours** are usually Monday–Friday 9am–4/4.30pm.

Children

Copenhagen is peaceful and safe, with plenty of sights and activities to keep kids amused. Most museums have excellent children's sections, and generally don't charge for under-18s; other attractions offer reduced rates. Highchairs and child-sized portions are widely available in cafés and restaurants.

Bakken funfair

As well as central sights such as Tivoli (see page 79), there are several major family attractions lying just outside Copenhagen which are well worth visiting.

Bakken and Bellevue Beach

The world's oldest funfair, Bakken (www.bakken.dk; April–August) attracts 2.5 million visitors a year during its short opening season with rides, sideshows and circus acts. The funfair is set in Dyrehaven, a lovely forested deer park just a short train ride north of Copenhagen. Alight at Klampenborg, from where the park is a ten-minute walk. Another big family attraction at Klampenborg is

Waterside Copenhagen in winter

the white-sand Bellevue Beach, two minutes' walk from the station.

Experimentarium

Located in an impressive modern building, the interactive science centre Experimentarium (Tuborg Havnevej 7, DK-2900 Hellerup; www.experimentarium.dk; charge), based north of the city in Hellerup, has sixteen interactive installations spread across two floors, and a roof terrace for outdoor activities.

National Aquarium Denmark (Den Blå Planet)

Northern Europe's largest aquarium (Danmarks Akvarium; Jacob Fortlingsvej 1; www.denblaaplanet.dk; charge) is located out near the airport at Amager. From the city centre, hop on the 5A bus towards Lufthavnen, alighting at the stop Den Blå Planet, from where the aquarium is a 200-metre/yd walk; or take the metro line M2 to Kastrup, then walk 600 metres/yds down Alleen in an easterly direction. There is also shuttle bus (free with ticket to the aquarium or Copenhagen Card) leaving every 45 minutes from various stops in the city centre (April–August), see website for details.

Climate

Copenhagen is on the same latitude as Moscow and Edinburgh, but the Gulf Stream has a modifying effect on the climate, making it mild for such a northerly city. The winter months, December to February, are cold and windy and there are only five hours of daylight. February is the coldest month with an average daytime temperature of 1.9°C (35°F), August the warmest at 20.4°C (69°F). In summer there are between sixteen and eighteen hours of daylight on a clear day.

You can check the latest weather forecasts for Copenhagen and the rest of the country on the Danish Meteorological Institute's website, www dmi.dk.

Crime and safety

Copenhagen is one of the least dangerous cities you could visit. However, it's never a bad thing to secure your personal possessions and not to take any personal risks. Be particularly aware of pickpocketing in crowded areas, such as around Central Station, Rådhuspladsen and the beginning of Strøget (the pedestrian street).

If you are victim of crime, the police are very efficient. **Main police station:** Politigården, tel: 33 14 88 88 or tel: 114.

Customs regulations

Visitors arriving from EU countries can bring reasonable amounts of cigarettes and spirits as long as it is for personal use. Visitors arriving

The Islands Brygge outdoor pool

from outside the EU can bring in two hundred cigarettes (or one hundred cigarillos, fifty cigars or 250g of tobacco) and 1 litre of spirits (or 2 litres of fortified wine or 4 litres of table wine or 16 litres of beer).

Food articles that are not vacuum-packed by the manufacturer cannot be brought into Denmark. If you are taking money (of any currency) worth over 10,000 euros in or out of the country, you must fill out a customs form.

Non-EU visitors travelling to a non-EU country are eligible for tax refunds: if you have spent over 300dkk in a single shop, ask the cashier for a tax-free form and get it stamped by customs on leaving the country. **Global Blue** (www.global blue.com), which has desks in the airport, will refund around twenty percent of the purchase price.

Electricity

220 volts AC (50 Hz) is the Danish standard. If you are travelling with electrical or electronic devices, be sure to bring a two-pin continental adapter with you.

Embassies and consulates

Australia: Dampfærgevej 26, 2nd Floor; tel: 70 26 36 76; www.denmark.embassy.gov.au.
Canada: Kristen Bernikowsgade 1; tel: 33 48 32 00; www.international.gc.ca.
Republic of Ireland: Østbanegade 21; tel: 35 47 32 00; www.dfa.ie/irish-embassy/denmark.
UK: Kastelsvej 36/38/40; tel: 35 44 52 00; www.gov.uk/world/organisations/british-embassy-copenhagen.
USA: Dag Hammarskjölds Allé 24; tel: 33 41 71 00; https://dk.usembassy.gov.

Emergencies

Emergency services (police, fire, ambulance): 112.
Politivagten (local police, not emergencies): 114.
Airport police: 32 31 34 00.
Out-of-hours medical care: A 24hr, 365-day helpline staffed by nurses who can advise on medical questions, and tell you which emergency clinic has the shortest waiting time – tel: 1813. Always call that number prior to going to hospital.
Dental emergency: Tandlægevagten, Oslo Plads 14, is a walk-in centre for out-of-hours dental emergencies, open Monday–Friday 8am–9.30pm, Saturday and Sunday and public holidays 10am–noon. Cash payment only.

Festivals and events

For an up-to-the-minute guide to what's on, visit the tourist office (see page 132) or pick up a copy of *Copenhagen This Week*. For public holidays, see page 131.

A wintery view from the Round Tower

Copenhagen Pride Parade

February

Vinterjazz. Two weeks of winter jazz. http://jazz.dk.
Frost Festival. A month of pop/electronic gigs in unusual venues. http://frostfestival.dk.
Shrovetide. Parades and carnival festivities, centred around Rådhuspladsen and the Nationalmuseet. Also, at Dragør on Amager island.
Copenhagen Gin Festival. The world's largest gin festival, with over 450 varieties, descends on a different venue each year.

March

CPH:DOX. A documentary film festival. https://cphdox.dk.

April

Queen's birthday. Crowds gather on 16 April outside Amalienborg Slot at noon for a balcony appearance.
Sakura Festival. Copenhagen Cherry Blossom Festival is a celebration of Japanese culture. https://sakurafestival.dk.

May

May Day. Marches and brass bands converge on Fælled Park.
Copenhagen Marathon. Runners pound the streets in mid-May. www.copenhagenmarathon.dk.
Distortion. Around 300,000 ravers join a city-wide party (late May/ early June). www.cphdistortion.dk.
3 Days of Design. Discover what's new in lifestyle, lightning and interiors at this three-day design festival. http://3daysofdesign.dk.

June

Copenhagen Carnival. Colourful Latin-style processions and hundreds of bands during the Whitsun Holiday.
St Hans Eve. Bonfires in parks and on beaches mark the longest day (23 June).
Roskilde Festival. Northern Europe's biggest rock festival takes place in late June/early July. www.roskilde-festival.dk.

July

Copenhagen Jazz Festival. Bebop and beyond, on stages, in pubs and on the streets. http://jazz.dk.

Christmas at Tivoli

Opera Festival. A week-long celebration of opera with open-air performances and concerts (ends first week of Aug). http://operafestival.dk.

August

Copenhagen Historic Grand Prix. Vintage cars rally. www.chgp.dk.
Copenhagen Pride. Five-day LGBTQ+ event culminating in a colourful parade. http://copenhagenpride.dk.
Copenhagen Summer Festival. The city's finest classical music festival, with top-drawer performers from around the world. www.copenhagensummerfestival.dk.

September

Golden Days Festival. Commemorates different eras of Copenhagen's history with cultural events. http://goldendaysfestival.dk.
Copenhagen Beer & Whisky Festival. A weekend of fun for whisky, beer, rum and gin fans as well as for foodies.

October

Culture Night. Museums, galleries, churches and theatres open their doors to the public after dark. www.kulturnatten.dk.
Blues Festival. Two weeks of concerts across the city. www.copenhagenbluesfestival.dk.

November–December

Tivoli Christmas Market. Tivoli transforms into a winter wonderland.

Health

The Danish medical system will assist anyone in an emergency; however, you should take out travel insurance before you leave. British nationals should take a Global Health Insurance Card (GHIC; https://overseas-healthcare.nhsbsa.nhs.uk). Emergency hospital treatment is free, as long as you have not travelled to Denmark intending to receive treatment and are too ill to return home.

Prescription drugs for personal use (thirty days' worth for Schengen residents, fifteen days' worth for non-Schengen visitors) may be brought to Denmark: try to bring along your doctor's prescription too. Pharmacies are designated by a green 'A' for Apotek. General opening hours are 9am–5.30pm and until 1pm on Sat. **Late-night opening:** Steno Apotek (24 hours); Vesterbrogade 6C (opposite main station); tel: 33 14 82 66.

LGBTQ+ travellers

Denmark was the first country to recognise same-sex marriages and is a welcoming place for LGBTQ+ travellers. For advice and information, contact **LGBT Danmark** (www.lgbt.dk). *Out & About* magazine (http://oaonline.dk) features listings for queer bars, nightlife and events, including Copenhagen Pride (www.copenhagenpride.dk) in mid-August. Copenhagen Gay

Life (www.patroc.com/copenhagen) is another good resource.

Lost property

For items lost on the bus, visit https://dinoffentligetransport.dk, click 'Kundeservice', then 'Hittegods' followed by 'Efterlys hittegods', then type in the bus number or metro or train to find the correct contact telephone number. Items lost on the local (S) train are kept for one month before being handed over to the police: tel: 48 29 87 00. For lost property at the airport, tel: 32 31 22 84. For all other losses, ring the police station at Slotsherrensvej 113; tel: 38 74 88 22.

Maps

The tourist board and most hotels offer free city maps marked with sights and sometimes bus routes. The Discover Green Copenhagen map, available in tourist offices, shows eco-friendly restaurants, bars and activities. If you need a street index, the Insight Copenhagen Fleximap is a good option.

Media

Newspapers and magazines: English-language newspapers and magazines are widely available. The English-language weekly *Copenhagen Post* (www.cphpost.dk; free from tourist offices and some hotels) has local news and listings. Denmark's main newspapers are *Berlingske Tidende*, *Ekstra Bladet*, *Jyllands-Posten* and *Politiken*.

Television: Cable and satellite television is widely available. Foreign films are rarely dubbed into Danish and appear in the original version with subtitles.

Money

Cash machines

ATMs are open 24 hours and can usually be found outside banks and metro stations. The smallest amount that you can draw out is 100dkk.

Credit cards

Visa, Mastercard and American Express are widely accepted but usually attract a fee. If your credit card gets lost or stolen, call the Danish PBS/Nets 24-hour hotline, tel: 44 89 27 50, to block your card.

Currency

Denmark uses Danish kroner (dkk). One krone is divided into 100 øre. Danish notes come in 1,000dkk, 500dkk, 200dkk, 100dkk and 50dkk. Coins are in denominations of 20dkk, 10dkk, 5dkk 2dkk, 1dkk, and 50 *øre* (half a krone).

Tax

Danish VAT is called MOMS and is set at 25 percent. It's always included in the bill. Non-EU visitors can

View of central Copenhagen at night

claim a tax refund if they spend over 300dkk in a single shop displaying the Global Tax-Free Shopping sign. Ask the cashier for a tax-free form, then take it to Tax Free Worldwide (www.taxfreeworldwide.com) or Global Blue (www.global-blue.com) desks in the airport and large department stores for a twenty percent refund. Alternatively, you can post your tax-free form.

Public and school holidays

Though Denmark's banks, offices and major shops close on public holidays, museums, cafés and tourist attractions will mostly be open. Christmas Eve and New Year's Eve are not official holidays, but most shops, businesses and attractions close on those days too. For festivals, see page 127.

1 January *Nytårsdag* New Year's Day
5 June (half-day) *Grundslovsdag* Constitution Day
25/26 December Christmas
Moveable dates (according to where Easter falls):
Skærtorsdag **Maundy Thursday**
Langfredag **Good Friday**
Anden påskedag **Easter Monday**
Store Bededag **General Prayer Day (fourth Friday after Easter)**
Kristi himmelfartsdag **Ascension Day**
Anden pinsedag **Whit Monday**

Religion

Denmark's Constitution provides for freedom of religion. The evangelical Lutheran church is the state church. Officially, 76 percent of Danes are members, but church attendance is low, and many Danes are agnostic or atheist. Muslims make up the second-largest religious community (three percent of the population).

Telephones

Local Danish numbers have eight digits. There are no area codes.
Local directory assistance: 118.
International directory assistance: 113.
International calls from Denmark: 00 + country code + area code + personal number.
International calls to Denmark: 00 + 45 + personal number.
International country codes: Britain +44, France +33, Germany +49, Ireland +353, Italy +39, Japan +81, Norway +47, Sweden +46, USA +1.
Public telephones: These are becoming scarce. Those left take pre-paid cards, available from kiosks, supermarkets and petrol stations; some take credit cards and coins (but not 50 øre coins). No change is given. Collect calls to the US are not possible.
Mobile telephones: Danish mobile phones operate on the 900/1800 Mhz GSM network, on which most unlocked European phones will work. US visitors will only be able to use their cellphone in Denmark if it is a tri-band phone that can switch bands.

Time zones

Denmark is one hour ahead of GMT. Summertime, when the clocks go forward one hour, runs from the last Sunday in March to the last Sunday in October.

Tourist information

The **Copenhagen Visitor Center** office (Vesterbrogade 4; tel: 70 22 24 42; www.visitcopenhagen.com; www.visitdenmark.dk) is opposite the Tivoli entrance. Staff speak English and there is free wi-fi. You can also purchase the Copenhagen Card from here. The tourist office has produced an official app, iSpot Copenhagen (available on iTunes and Google Play), with lots of information plus a current events calendar.

A **Copenhagen Card** (CPH Card; www.copenhagencard.com) gives entry to eighty-plus attractions in the Copenhagen area, offers discounts and also entitles you to free travel on trains, buses and the metro (this includes public transport to/from the airport, and also to Roskilde, Helsingør and the art galleries in Tour 14). They are valid for 24hr, 48hr, 72hr and 120hr, and up to two children under the age of 10 are allowed free with each adult card. You can buy the cards online or at the tourist office, airport and main railway stations.

The English newspaper, ***Copenhagen Post*** (published on Fridays) has a useful weekly guide to what's on.

Transport

Getting to Copenhagen is easy, with many airlines offering daily flights, as well as direct rail services from Sweden and Germany. Access from the airport is also very straightforward with train, bus and taxi options, which will take you to the city centre. There are also ferry services to Copenhagen.

Getting there

By plane

Budget airlines offering flights to Copenhagen include easyJet (www.easyjet.com) and Norwegian (www.norwegian.com). Copenhagen Airport, Kastrup (www.cph.dk) lies 12km (7.5 miles) southeast of the city centre, on Amager Island. There are trains to Hovedbanegård, Copenhagen's Central Station; and the metro runs roughly every four to six minutes (15–20min at night) into the city centre. Both leave from Terminal 3 (where all passengers go for baggage reclaim and customs) and take about fourteen minutes. Bus 5A operates every ten minutes during the day and connects the airport with the city centre.

There is a **taxi rank** at Terminal 3. The twenty-minute taxi journey to the centre costs around 300–400dkk depending on the time and includes VAT and tip.

Copenhagen is one of Europe's most cycle-friendly cities

By train

There are up to five direct trains daily to/from Hamburg, Germany; and trains run every ten minutes to/from Sweden (Gothenburg, Malmö and Stockholm), arriving at Hovedbanegård (Central Station). The S-tog (local) trains also leave from the Central Station and run on a separate network.

For German rail enquiries and bookings, contact **DB Bahn** (www.bahn.de).

For Swedish rail journeys, contact **SJ** (www.sj.se).

For Danish and outgoing international rail enquiries and bookings, contact **Danish Rail** (DSB; www.dsb.dk).

By bus

The biggest operator of scheduled coach services to/from Denmark is FlixBus (www.flixbus.com). Buses stop at Copenhagen's Central Station.

By ferry

The new ferry terminal, close to Nordhavn train station, is linked to the city centre by shuttle bus. **DFDS Seaways** (Denmark; www.dfdsseaways.com) operates ferries from Oslo (16hr) to Copenhagen. Ferries from Germany with **Scandlines** (www.scandlines.com) arrive at Rødby, Elsinore and Gedser.

By cruise ship

Cruise ships dock at one of four cruise terminals – Langelinie Quay, Nordre Toldbod, Freeport (Frihavnen) and Ocean Quay (Oceankaj) – all in the north harbour (Nordhavn). You can walk into the city along the waterside, or bus No. 26 links the terminals with the Central Station, Rådhuspladsen (City Hall Square) and Kongens Nytorv.

DFDS Seaways ferry

By car

Drivers arriving in Rødby from Germany (Puttgarden) should take the E47. Both the Storebælt bridge/tunnel from Funen to Sjælland, and the Øresund bridge from Malmö to Copenhagen levy a toll.

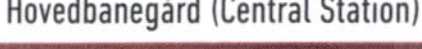

Hovedbanegård (Central Station)

Getting around

For fare purposes, the city is divided into zones. Fares are charged on the number of zones that you pass through (minimum two).

The bus, harbour bus, metro and S-tog (local train) all use the same tickets so you can change between them without buying a new one. The cheapest options are to buy a Copenhagen Card or a Citypass (see page 132), with which local travel is free.

Tickets can be bought on the bus, at ticket offices or vending machines. Discount cards, with an average saving of forty percent, cannot be bought on the bus. At the time of writing the price of a single ticket (adult) for one zone was 34dkk.

By bus

Buses are operated by Movia (www.moviatrafik.dk). They are regular, although the city is so compact that it's usually easier to walk. Nearly all stop at either Rådhuspladsen (City Hall Square) or Hovedbanegård (Central Station).

Buses run daily between 6am and 12.30am and there are additional night buses from Rådhuspladsen (City Hall Square) to the suburbs.

Buses are yellow and you get on at the front and off at the back.

By S-tog

The S-tog (local train) connects Copenhagen with other towns on Sjælland. Tickets are available at all S-tog stations.

By metro

The award-winning driverless metro (www.m.dk) operates a frequent service: every three to six minutes in the daytime, and every fifteen to twenty minutes through the night. Currently, there are four lines. From Vanløse Station, M1 runs to West Amager, while M2 runs to Copenhagen Airport in East Amager. Both lines take you through the heart of the city. M3 loops in a circle around the city, connecting seventeen stations, and M4 connects Nordhavn in the north with the southern terminus of Sydhavn.

By bicycle

The Danes are avid cyclists and bicycles enjoy equal status with cars on Copenhagen's roads. When using the cycleways, keep to the right. Helmets are optional, but cycling without lights at night, under the influence of alcohol or jumping red lights can earn you an instant 700dkk fine.

You can join in by borrowing one of Copenhagen's electric, puncture-free, GPS-fitted **Bycyklen** (www.bycyklen.dk), available at various docking stations around the inner city for 30dkk a hour. You will need to set up an account via the website before you travel. Bicycles are widely available from hostels, hotels and private hire shops, with rental varying from free to 80–150dkk per day; 270–530dkk per week.

A busy cycle lane

Bike-rental companies include **beCopenhagen** (Fortunstræde 1; https://becopenhagen.dk) and **Baisikeli** (Turesensgade 10; http://baisikeli.dk), which uses its profits to ship bicycles – over five thousand at the last count – to Mozambique. **Bike Copenhagen with Mike** (https://bikecopenhagenwithmike.dk) operates cycling tours of the city.

By harbour bus

The blue-and-yellow harbour buses follow two routes. The 991/992 sails from Refshaleøen to Teglholmen, in the southwest, stopping at the Black Diamond, Knippel's Bridge (Christianshavn), Nyhavn and the Opera House. The 993 zips between Nyhavn and the Opera House. Harbour buses run daily from 6am–6/7pm, and accept local transport tickets. They are free with the Copenhagen Card.

By car

Cars are not practical in Copenhagen, but if you do hire a car, you must be over 20 years old and hold a valid licence. Some car firms may stipulate that you have to be over 25.

Danes drive on the right and speed limits are 130kmh (66 or 80mph) on motorways, 80kmh (50mph) on other roads and 50kmh (30mph) in a built-up area. Take a UK or EU driving licence and a warning triangle, and always wear a seatbelt.

Headlights must be dipped at all times. Be aware of cycle lanes on both sides of the road in towns. *Parkering Forbudt* means 'No Parking'.

Copenhagen is comparatively well equipped for electric vehicles. Most of the rental companies below offer electric cars, and there are charging points across the city – a map can be found at https://chargemap.com/cities/copenhagen-DK.

Car-hire companies

Budget: www.budget.dk

Sixt: www.sixt.dk

Taxis

Taxis can be identified by the sign on the roof with the word FRI, meaning 'free'. Most drivers speak English and often some German. They can give you receipts, and you can pay with a credit card. The basic fare for a taxi is 40dkk, then 15.25dkk for each kilometre. Tips are not expected, but it is usual to round up the final amount.

Dantaxi: tel: 70 25 25 25; www.dantaxi.dk/Koebenhavn.

Taxa 4x35: tel: 35 35 35 35. Also provides taxis equipped with wheelchair lifts and ramps for disabled passengers (tel: 35 35 35 35; www.taxa.dk).

Visas

EU citizens do not need a visa; other visitors should check with their country. Visitors not obliged to have a visa are allowed to stay in Denmark for up to ninety days. See www.nyidanmark.dk.

Copenhagen's bright yellow buses are easy to spot

Language

English is widely spoken and understood. Danish is perhaps the most difficult Northern European language for relating the written word to speech; it's almost impossible to pronounce simply by reading the words, as many syllables are swallowed rather than spoken. Thus, the island of Amager becomes Am-air, with the 'g' disappearing, but in a distinctively Danish way difficult for the visitor to imitate. The letter 'd' becomes something like a 'th', but with the tongue placed behind the lower teeth, not the upper. And the letter 'r' is, again, swallowed. Despite their differences of grammar, usage and vocabulary, Danes, Norwegians and Swedes are able to understand one another.

Vowels

a – aa, as in bar
å – aw, as in paw
æ – as in pear
e – as in bed
i – ee, as in sleep
ø – as in fur

Useful words and phrases

General

yes/no *ja/nej*
big/little *stor/lille*
good/bad *god/dårlig*
possible/impossible *muligt/umuligt*
hot/cold *varm/kold*
much/little *meget/lidt*
many/few *mange/få*
and/or *og/eller*
please/thank you *vær så venlig/tak*
I *jeg*
you (formal) *du (de)*
he/she *han/hun*
it *den/det*
we *vi*
you (formal) *I (de)*
they *de*
foreigner *udlænding*

Numbers

1 *en/et*
2 *to*
3 *tre*
4 *fire*
5 *fem*
6 *seks*
7 *syv*
8 *otte*
9 *ni*
10 *ti*
20 *tyve*
30 *tredive*
40 *fyrre*
50 *halvtreds*
60 *tres*
70 *halvfjerds*
80 *firs*
90 *halvfems*
100 *hundrede*

The sleek Royal Danish Playhouse

Food and drink

breakfast *morgenmad*
lunch (break) *frokost (pause)*
dinner *middag*
tea *te*
coffee *kaffe*
beer *fadøl*

Getting around

left *venstre*
right *højre*
street *(en) gade/vej*
bicycle (path) *(en) cykel (sti)*
car *(en) bil*
bus/coach *(en) bus*
train *(et) tog*
ferry *(en) færge*
bridge *(en) bro*
traffic light *(et) trafiklys*
square *(et) torv*
north *nord*
south *syd*
east *øst*
west *vest*

Money

How much is it? *Hvad koster det?*
Can I pay with… *Må jeg betale med…*
travellers' cheques *rejsechecks*
money *penge*
notes/coins *sedler/mønter*
Please may I have *Må jeg få*
the bill? *regningen?*
May I have a *Må jeg få en*
receipt? *kvittering?*
bank *(en) bank*
exchange *veksle*
exchange rate *kurs*
business hours *åbningstider*
open *åben*
closed *lukket*

Medical

pharmacy *(et) apotek*
hospital *(et) hospital*
casualty *(en) skadestue*
doctor *(en) læge*

Time

What time is it? *Hvad er klokken?*
good morning *godmorgen*
good day/evening *goddag*
goodnight *godaften/godnat*
today *i dag*
tomorrow *i morgen*

Calendar

Monday *mandag*
Tuesday *tirsdag*
Wednesday *onsdag*
Thursday *torsdag*
Friday *fredag*
Saturday *lørdag*
Sunday *søndag*
January *januar*
February *februar*
March *marts*
April *april*
May *maj*
June *juni*
July *juli*
August *august*
September *september*
October *oktober*
November *november*
December *december*

Food festivals are a great place to meet the locals

Books and film

The Danes have always been a nation of storytellers: as far back as the third century, runes proclaimed the deeds of warriors and kings. In the thirteenth century, Saxo Grammaticus created Denmark's first major literary work, *Gesta Danorum* (*History of the Danes*), which inspired Shakespeare's *Hamlet*. During the Danish Golden Age (1800–50), Hans Christian Andersen strode the world stage and Søren Kierkegaard wrestled with the meaning of life. The best-known authors of modern times are Karen Blixen and former ballet-dancer Peter Høeg.

Homegrown Danish cinema really took off during World War II, when the occupying Germans banned the import of foreign films. In the 1990s, in protest against overblown Hollywood productions, Lars von Trier and Thomas Vinterberg launched the Dogme 95 manifesto, whose rigid and complex rules were paradoxically used to create simple, naturalistic films.

Books

History

A History of the Vikings by Gwyn Jones. A compelling history of Viking society.

The Vikings by Else Roesdahl. Another good exploration of the Norse traders, raiders and explorers.

The Battle of Copenhagen 1801 by Ole Feldbæk. How Napoleonic politics led to the brutal bombardment of Copenhagen by the British.

The English Dane: From King of Iceland to Tasmanian Convict by Sarah Bakewell. A fascinating account of arch-blagger Jorgen Jorgenson, the self-appointed King of Iceland.

Danish Dynamite: The Story of Football's Greatest Cult Team by Rob Smyth, Lars Eriksen and Mike Gibbons. Tracing the rise of the coolest football team on earth.

Non-fiction

Out of Africa by Karen Blixen (aka Isak Dinesen). Vivid autobiography of a Danish aristocrat, later made into a Hollywood film starring Meryl Streep.

Early Spring by Tove Ditlevsen. A funny, poignant account of growing up in working-class Vesterbro in the 1920s.

Either/Or, Fear and Trembling and ***The Concept of Anxiety*** by Søren Kierkegaard. Ponder the imponderables with Denmark's favourite existentialist philosopher.

Quantum: Einstein, Bohr and the Great Debate About the Nature of Reality by Manjit Kumar. A rollicking read, focusing on a decades-long argument between Einstein and Nobel-Prize-winning physicist Niels Bohr.

A model of Hans Christian Andersen at his writing desk

Danish Modern by Andrew Hollingsworth. A history of Danish design, from the eighteenth century to the present.

Fiction

The Complete Fairy Tales by Hans Christian Andersen. Classic childhood tales, such as 'The Little Mermaid' and 'The Ugly Duckling'.
The Exception by Christian Jungersen. A bestselling psychological thriller, told from four different viewpoints.
The Visit of The Royal Physician by Per Olov Enquist. Madness, passion and intrigue in the eighteenth-century Danish court.
The History of Danish Dreams by Peter Høeg. A magical-realist account of Denmark's transition to a modern state.
Silence in October by Jens Christian Grøndahl. The end of a marriage brings dark reflections in this stream-of-consciousness novel.
We, the Drowned by Carsten Jensen. This brilliant novel follows three generations of sailors from the Danish town of Marstal.

Film and TV

Babette's Feast (Babettes Gæstebud), 1987, dir. Gabriel Axel. Sumptuous Oscar-winning film based on a short story by Karen Blixen, set in Jutland.
Pelle the Conqueror (Pelle Erobreren), 1987, dir. Bille August. Award-winning film about a Swedish father and son immigrating to Bornholm.
Breaking the Waves, 1996, dir. Lars von Trier. A psychologically damaged Scottish woman is urged by her husband to have sex with other men after an accident leaves him paralysed.
Festen, 1996, dir. Thomas Vinterberg. Family secrets emerge at a birthday celebration. The first film made using Dogme 95 rules.
The Idiots (Idioterne), 1998, dir. Lars von Trier. A group of Copenhageners test the boundaries of 'normality' in a Dogme 95 film that still has the power to shock.
After the Wedding (Efter Brylluppet), 2007, dir. Susanne Bier. Oscar-nominated film about a Danish director of an Indian orphanage.
A Royal Affair (En kongelig affære), 2012, dir. Nikolaj Arcel. Superb historical drama about the affair between Johann Struensee and Queen Caroline Matilda.
A Hijacking (Kapringen), 2012, dir. Tobias Lindholm. A Danish freighter is captured by Somali pirates in this ultra-tense hostage drama.
Men and chicken (Mænd & høns), 2015, dir. Anders Thomas Jensen. Award-wining tale about two brothers discovering a terrifying family secret.
The Man (Mesteren), 2017, dir. Charlotte Sieling. A fascinating story about a complicated father-son rivalry.
The Promised Land (Bastarden), 2023, dir. Nikolaj Arcel. Historical epic about the eighteenth-century settlement of Jutland.

Susanne Bier receiving an Oscar for her 2010 film, *In a Better World (Hævnen)*

About this book

The Rough Guides Walks & Tours series helps you discover the world's most exciting destinations through our expert-curated trip plans: a range of walks and tours designed to suit all budgets, interests and trip lengths. These walks, driving tours and site excursions cover the destination's most quintessential attractions as well as a range of lesser-known sights, while food and drink stops for refreshments en route are highlighted in boxes. If you're not sure which walk to pick, our Best walks & tours for... feature suggests which ones work best for particular interests. The introduction provides a destination overview, while the directory supports the walks and tours with all the essential information you need, as well as our pick of where to stay while you are there and select restaurant listings, to complement the more low-key options given in the trip plans.

About the authors

Antonia Cunningham has written several books, including two books on world art and the Impressionists, and five on Copenhagen and Denmark. She lives in London with her partner Nick and son Benjamin, to both of whom she dedicates this book. This edition was updated by Dan Stables, a Manchester-based travel writer who writes articles for *National Geographic Traveller* and the BBC, and his debut narrative travel book, *Fiesta: A Journey Through Festivity* is coming out in early 2026. He also hosts a podcast, Hungry Ghosts, about food and travel. You can find his work on X @DanStables, Instagram @DanStabs, or at www.danielstables.co.uk.

Help us update

We've gone to a lot of effort to ensure that this edition of the **Rough Guides Walks & Tours Copenhagen** is accurate and up-to-date. However, things change – places get "discovered", new gems open up, restaurants and rooms raise prices or lower standards. If you feel we've got it wrong or left something out, we'd like to know, and if you can remember the address, the website, whether or not it was free to enter – so much the better.

Please send your comments with the subject line "**Rough Guides Walks & Tours Copenhagen Update**" to mail@roughguides.com. We'll acknowledge all contributions and send a copy of the next edition (or any other Rough Guide if you prefer) for the very best emails.

Credits

Rough Guides Walks & Tours Copenhagen
Editors: Rachel Lawrence, Joanna Reeves
Author: Daniel Stables
Picture Editor: Piotr Kala
Picture Manager: Tom Smyth
Cartography: Katie Bennett
Layout: Grzegorz Madejak
Production Operations Manager: Katie Bennett
Publishing Technology Manager: Rebeka Davies
Head of Publishing: Sarah Clark
Photo credits: All images Shutterstock except: Alastair Wiper/Kødbyens Fiskebar 116T; Apa Publications 63; Carlsberg 33R; David Hall/Apa Publications 36/37, 133, 135; Hôtel d'Angleterre 45; Ib Rasmussen 42; iStock 1, 6CT, 7CT, 14/15, 44, 46/47, 52, 53R, 55R, 71, 74, 78, 92, 125; Kiin Ny 119T; Nimb Brasserie 115T; Rudy Hemmingsen/Apa Publications 7CB, 22, 32/33, 34, 36, 37R, 38, 40, 40/41, 46, 47R, 50, 51R, 52/53, 54, 54/55, 56, 58, 58/59, 59R, 60, 60/61, 61R, 72, 72/73, 73R, 75, 76, 77, 78/79, 79R, 80, 81, 82, 83R, 82/83, 84, 84/85, 85R, 86, 86/87, 87R, 88, 88/89, 89R, 90, 91, 93, 94, 94/95, 95R, 96, 97, 98, 99, 100, 101B, 102, 102/103; SMK Foto 62, 64, 65B, 66T, 66B, 67; VEGA 23; Wonderful Copenhagen 6T, 6CB, 6B, 7T, 7B, 8/9, 10, 11, 12, 13R, 12/13, 16, 17R, 16/17, 18, 19, 20, 21, 24, 30, 32, 35, 38/39, 39R, 41R, 48, 49, 50/51, 69, 70B, 70T, 103R, 106, 106/107, 107R, 108, 108/109B, 109B, 110, 110/111B, 111B, 112, 112/113B, 113B, 114, 115B, 116B, 116/117, 117R, 118, 119B, 120, 121, 122, 122/123, 123B, 124, 126, 127, 128/129, 130/131, 132, 134, 136, 137
Cover credits: Clock in Kultorvet **iStock**

Printed by Elma Basim in Turkey

This book was produced using **Typefi** automated publishing software.

A catalogue record for this book is available from the British Library.

First Edition 2025

ISBN: 9781835292419

Distribution

UK, Ireland and Europe
Apa Publications (UK) Ltd
mail@roughguides.com
United States and Canada
Two Rivers
ips@ingramcontent.com
Australia and New Zealand
Woodslane
info@woodslane.com.au
Worldwide
Apa Publications (UK) Ltd
mail@roughguides.com

Special Sales, Content Licensing and CoPublishing

Rough Guides can be purchased in bulk quantities at discounted prices. We can create special editions, personalized jackets and corporate imprints tailored to your needs.
mail@roughguides.com
http://roughguides.com

EU Representative

LOGOS EUROPE, 9 rue Nicolas Poussin, 17000, LA ROCHELLE, France
Contact@logoseurope.eu; +33 (0) 667937378

Index

J

K

L

M

N

O

P

Q

R

MAP LEGEND

- Start of tour
- Tour & route direction
- Recommended sight
- Recommended restaurant/café
- Place of interest
- Tourist information
- Statue/monument
- Main post office
- Main bus station
- Viewpoint
- Park
- Important building
- Hotel
- Transport hub
- Market/store
- Pedestrian area
- Urban area